Get INVOLVED!

Student's Book
with Digital Student's Book

Gill Holley   Kate Pickering

Get INVOLVED!

Collaborative projects

Collaborate with your classmates to develop your problem-solving skills in the WDYT? projects. Become an expert on a topic and get involved with others in your class.

WDYT?
(What do you think?)

Real-world content

Learn about culture while you learn English. *Get Involved!* is full of real-world content, so go online and learn more about the people, events and places in the book.

Super skills

Get Involved! helps develop your critical thinking, collaboration, creativity and communication skills, which are essential for life in the 21st century.

COLLABORATION

CRITICAL THINKING

SUPER SKILLS

COMMUNICATION

CREATIVITY

Building skills for the real world

Social and emotional learning

Get Involved! helps you develop strategies to deal with social situations and gives you the vocabulary you need to discuss emotions that you or others experience.

Media-rich content

Get Involved! videos help you with critical thinking, communication and project presentations and improve your video literacy skills.
Access On-the-Go Practice on your phone through the Macmillan Student's App and improve your English with gamified content.

Inclusive classroom

Show your strengths and talents by putting your investigative skills and logic to the test with *Get Involved!* Brain teasers. Learn at your own pace with graded Workbook activities and The longer read.

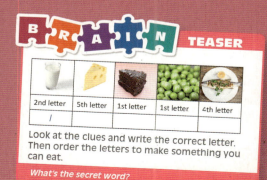

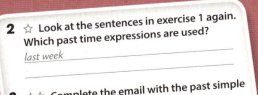

2 ☆ Look at the sentences in exercise 1 again. Which past time expressions are used?
last week

3 ☆☆ Complete the email with the past simple form of the verbs in the box.

UNIT	VOCABULARY	GRAMMAR	READING AND CRITICAL THINKING
STARTER What do you know? Page 6	**Vocabulary:** countries and nationalities, in the classroom, family, describing people, action verbs		
1 School life **WDYT?** What is an ideal school? Page 12	Daily routines School subjects ▶ Japanese school life	Present simple: affirmative and negative Present simple: Yes/No questions Object pronouns	**An online article** *A day in the life of an online student* **Subskill:** Predicting from the title and the pictures
2 Me time **WDYT?** How important are hobbies for teenagers? Page 24	Free-time activities Collocations with *do*, *go* and *play* ▶ My time	Adverbs of frequency Likes and dislikes Present simple: *Wh-* questions	**A blog** *At the top of her game* **Subskill:** Reading for specific information
3 Dressing up **WDYT?** Why do people dress up? Page 36	Clothes and accessories Describing clothes ▶ The art of fashion	Present continuous Present simple and present continuous Time expressions	**A live feed** *Comic Con* **Subskill:** Identifying the text type
4 Extremes **WDYT?** How does the weather affect the way we live? Page 48	Seasons and weather Compound nouns: things to take on a trip ▶ Four seasons in a week	Comparative and superlative adjectives Modal verbs of obligation, permission and prohibition	**A magazine article** *Our amazing world* **Subskill:** Understanding the main idea
5 Must try! **WDYT?** What makes a town a good place to live in? Page 60	Food and drink Places in a town ▶ Picnic snack ideas	Countable and uncountable nouns *there is/are* *Is there …? Are there …?* *How much/many …?*	**A guidebook** *How to eat like a local* **Subskill:** Identifying key words
6 Animals in danger **WDYT?** What can we do to help animals in danger? Page 72	Describing animals Collocations: taking action ▶ Top five animal videos	Past simple: *be* Past simple of regular verbs: affirmative and negative	**An article** *The saiga and the mountain gorilla* **Subskill:** Understanding the content of paragraphs
7 Heroes **WDYT?** What makes a hero? Page 84	Jobs Adjectives to describe people ▶ Formula 1, let's go!	Past simple of irregular verbs: affirmative and negative Past simple: question forms and *ago*	**A newspaper article** *Heroic teens* **Subskill:** Understanding new words
8 Summer fun **WDYT?** What's your idea of a good holiday? Page 96	Holidays Holiday activities ▶ Cool summer holidays	*will* for predictions Future with *going to* Present continuous for future arrangements	**A travel blog** *Sit back, get comfortable and … travel?* **Subskill:** Identifying facts and opinions
9 Look what you know! Page 108	**Vocabulary** and **Grammar** review		**Reading:** review of subskills

Pronunciation p116   Project planner p118

LISTENING	REAL-WORLD SPEAKING	WRITING	PRONUNCIATION	PROJECT
Grammar: *be* (affirmative, negative and questions), possessive adjectives, possessive *'s* and *s'*, *have got*, *can* for ability				
A conversation British and Finnish teenagers comparing their schools **Subskill:** Identifying the type of listening	▶ Working together to check answers	**A blog post** **Subskill:** Capital letters	Silent letters	▶ Design a timetable for your ideal school. **Critical thinking** Making logical decisions
A radio interview with a hockey player **Subskill:** Listening for the general idea	▶ Asking for information	**Informal messages** **Subskill:** *and*, *or* and *but*	*do you* /djʊ/	▶ Do a survey about how students in the class spend their free time. **Collaboration** Planning and task management
A live report about No Uniform Day **Subskill:** Listening to questions and answers	▶ Shopping for clothes	**Photo descriptions** **Subskill:** *because* and *so*	/n/ and /ŋ/	▶ Make a mini-book about traditional clothes. **Creativity** Using your imagination and thinking of original ideas
Instructions for an adventure holiday in Yosemite **Subskill:** Using pictures to help you understand	▶ Making and responding to suggestions	**Instructions** **Subskill:** *too* and *also*	*can*	▶ Make a video giving weather advice to visitors to your country. **Communication** Active listening
An informal conversation about a visit to Buenos Aires **Subskill:** Predicting vocabulary	▶ Asking for directions	**A description of a place** **Subskill:** Adjectives	/iː/ and /ɪ/	▶ Make a map showing useful places for young people moving to live in your town. **Critical thinking** Considering the needs of other people
A podcast about a teen entrepreneur **Subskill:** Identifying which statements are true or false	▶ Showing interest	**An email** **Subskill:** Sequencing words	Past simple endings /d/ /t/ /ɪd/	▶ Prepare a poster about endangered animals to raise awareness and help to protect them. **Collaboration** Listening to other people's opinions
A podcast about two talented teens **Subskill:** Listening for numbers	▶ Giving opinions	**A biography** **Subskill:** Writing in paragraphs	Schwa /ə/	▶ Make a digital presentation about a hero from the past. **Creativity** Using feedback to improve your work
Phone conversations and messages about holiday plans **Subskill:** Listening for feelings	▶ Making arrangements	**Invitations** **Subskill:** Apostrophes	*will*	▶ Create a three-day holiday plan for you and your friends. **Communication** Communicating clearly
Listening: review of subskills		**Speaking:** review of Key phrases		**Writing:** review of subskills

Phrasebook p122   Irregular verbs p126

STARTER — What do you know?

All around the world

Vocabulary: countries and nationalities

1 Copy and complete the table.

Country	Nationality	Country	Nationality
Australia	1 (…)	8 (…)	Mexican
2 (…)	Brazilian	Morocco	9 (…)
Canada	3 (…)	10 (…)	Nigerian
4 (…)	Chinese	Spain	11 (…)
France	5 (…)	12 (…)	Turkish
6 (…)	Irish	the UK	13 (…)
7 (…)	Japanese	14 (…)	American

2 1 Listen and check. Identify the stressed syllable.

Au**stra**lia – Au**stra**lian

3 Work in pairs. Complete the quiz with countries in exercise 1. You have three minutes!

Grammar: *be* (affirmative, negative and *Yes/No* questions)

4 Copy and complete the table with *is*, *isn't*, *are* and *aren't*.

Affirmative		Negative	
I'm	British.	I'm not	French.
You/We/They 1 (…)		You/We/They 3 (…)	
He/She/It 2 (…)		He/She/It 4 (…)	

5 Write affirmative or negative sentences. Add capital letters.

1 he / from 🇯🇵 (+) *He's from Japan.*
2 she / 🇮🇪 (-) *She isn't Irish.*
3 we / from 🇧🇷 (+)
4 it / 🇦🇺 (-)
5 I / 🇹🇷 (+)
6 you / from 🇳🇬 (-)

THE BIG WORLD QUIZ

1 Name three countries where people speak English.
2 Tokyo is the capital city of …
3 Name three countries in Europe.
4 Name two countries where people speak Spanish.
5 Say five countries with the letter 'r' in their names.
6 Name two countries in Africa.

Starter

6 Read the examples and choose the correct option to complete the rules.

Are you Spanish?	No, I'm not.
Are you Mexican?	Yes, I am.

1 For Yes/No questions, the verb be comes **first/second**.
2 For short answers in the affirmative, **use/don't use** contractions.
3 For short answers in the negative, **use/don't use** contractions.

7 Match questions 1–5 with answers a–e.

1 Is she a teacher?   a No, it isn't.
2 Are we on exercise 4? b Yes, she is.
3 Are they your pens?   c No, they aren't.
4 Is it the correct answer? d Yes, you are.
5 Am I in the right classroom? e No, we aren't.

Are you new here?
Vocabulary: in the classroom

1 🔊 2 Listen and write the letters. What words do you hear?

2 Complete the words with vowels to make classroom objects.

1 CL (...) CK   6 C (...) MP (...) T (...) R
2 B (...) (...) K   7 N (...) T (...) B (...) (...) K
3 P (...) NC (...) L 8 SH (...) RP (...) N (...) R
4 CH (...) (...) R   9 D (...) CT (...) (...) N (...) RY
5 B (...) (...) RD   10 W (...) ND (...) W

3 💬 Work in pairs. Point to something in the classroom and ask and answer the questions.

What's this?   It's a notebook.

> **this/these, that/those**
> Ask 'What's **this**?' (singular) and 'What are **these**?' (plural) for things near you.
> Ask 'What's **that**?' (singular) and 'What are **those**?' (plural) for things at a distance.

4 🔊 3 Listen to the instructions and match them with pictures a–f.

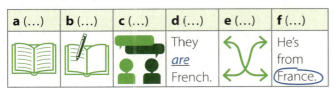

5 🔊 4 Listen and match conversations 1–4 with pictures A–D.

Grammar: be (Wh- questions)

6 Read the examples and choose the correct option in the rule.

What's this?	It's a pen.
What are those?	They're my books.

For Wh- questions, the verb comes **before/after** the question word.

7 Match the question words in the box with pictures 1–5.

| How old? | What? | When? | Where? | Who? |

1 (...)	2 (...)	3 (...)	4 (...)	5 (...)
🕐	📍	🧍	I'm 12.	🎁?

8 Order the words to make questions.

1 name / your / What's ?
2 you from / Where / are ?
3 are / How old / you ?
4 favourite sport / What's / your ?
5 your / favourite singer / Who's ?

9 💬 Work in pairs. Ask and answer the questions in exercise 8.

7

Starter

Families – big and small
Vocabulary: family

1 Copy and complete the table with the family words in the box.

> aunt ~~brother~~ cousin daughter father
> grandfather grandmother mother
> nephew niece parent sister son uncle

Male	Female	Both
brother		

2 Write the family member.
1 Your mother's brother *uncle*
2 Your father's mother
3 Your sister's son
4 Your mother's daughter
5 Your aunt's son

> mother and father = parents
> son and daughter = children

3 Work in pairs. Describe the families in the photos.

> I think this is the mother.
> Or maybe they're three sisters …

4 Match family descriptions 1–3 with photos A–D in exercise 3. There is one photo you don't need.

Families around the world
Some of our readers tell us about their families.

1 I live with my family in London. My dad's from India, and my aunts, uncles and cousins all live there. My dad's name is Samar and he's 45 years old. My mum's 39. Her name is Liz. I've got two sisters.

2 I've got three sisters. My older sister's married and she's got a son and a daughter. My nephew's name is Jia and my niece is called Fin. My grandmother lives with us. I've got six cousins.

3 I live with my mum and my sister. We're a small family, but we're close to our neighbours. They're called Mr and Mrs Evans and their sons' names are Caleb and Damien. They're like brothers to me.

5 Find 12 family members in the descriptions.

Grammar: possessive adjectives

6 Read the example. Copy and complete the table with the possessive adjectives in the box.

> **My** mum's 39. **Her** name is Liz.

> his its our their your

Subject pronouns	I	you	he	she	it	we	they
Possessive adjectives	my	1 (…)	2 (…)	her	3 (…)	4 (…)	5 (…)

7 Complete the sentences with possessive adjectives.
1 My grandfather is 70 years old. (…) name's Frank.
2 My cousins live with (…) parents in the USA.
3 We've got a big garden, but (…) house is small.
4 My sister lives with (…) husband and two children.
5 What about you? Is (…) family big or small?

Starter

Grammar: possessive 's and s'

> My nephew's name is Jia. (singular noun + 's)
> Their sons' names are Caleb and Damien. (plural noun ending in s + ')

8 Add one apostrophe (') to each sentence.
 1 My dads family is in India.
 2 My grandparents house is in Chennai.
 3 I see my cousins at my uncles house.
 4 My cousins names are Ajay and Hari.

Who is it?

Vocabulary: describing people

1 Find the people in the picture.

 1 He's got black hair and a moustache. He wears glasses. He hasn't got a beard.
 2 She's got short blonde hair and blue eyes.
 3 He's got fair hair. He hasn't got a beard.
 4 She's tall. She's got short curly hair and glasses.

2 Copy the table and add words from exercise 1.

General description	Hair	Hair colour	Eyes	Other
short	long	brown	brown	beard
	straight	grey	green	

3 🔊 5 Listen and match the descriptions to the people in exercise 1.

Grammar: have got

4 Copy and complete the table with *has*, *hasn't* or *haven't*.

	Affirmative	Negative
I/You/We/They	have got black hair.	1 (…) got blue eyes.
He/She/It	2 (…) got short hair.	3 (…) got glasses.

5 Complete the sentences with the correct form of *have got*.
 1 He (…) a beard and glasses. (+)
 2 They (…) any children. (-)
 3 I (…) a cat called Sam. (+)
 4 We (…) any cousins. (-)
 5 She (…) any brothers or sisters. (-)

6 Copy and complete the table with *has*, *hasn't*, *have* or *haven't*.

Questions	Short answers
Have you got curly hair?	Yes, I have./No, I 1 (…).
2 (…) he got a beard?	Yes, he has./No, he 3 (…).
Have they got blue eyes?	Yes, they 4 (…)./No, they haven't.

7 Write questions with *have got*.
 1 you / any brothers or sisters ?
 2 your dad / a beard ?
 3 your mum / long hair ?
 4 your parents / any brothers or sisters ?
 5 you / a lot of cousins ?

8 💬 Work in pairs. Ask and answer the questions in exercise 7. Then write a description of your partner's family.
Tania's got a big family. She's got two brothers …

9 Read the text and answer the question.

Two parents have got six sons. Each son has got a sister.

How many people are there in the family?

Starter

What can you do?
Vocabulary: action verbs

1 Match the words in the box with pictures 1–10.

> cook   dance   draw   play   ride   run
> sing   speak   spell   swim

(…) a bike

(…) the guitar

Nĭ hăo!

(…) Chinese

(…) fast

2 🔊 6 Listen. What is the verb? Can the people do the action?

1 *sing – yes*

Grammar: *can* for ability

3 Copy and complete the table with sentences a–d.
- a He can't spell.
- b Can they cook?
- c Yes, they can.
- d She can swim.

Affirmative	Negative
I can draw.	I can't sing.
1 (…)	2 (…)
They can speak Chinese.	They can't speak French.
Questions	**Short answers**
Can you play the guitar?	Yes, I can./No, I can't.
Can he sing?	Yes, he can./No, he can't.
3 (…)	4 (…) /No, they can't.

4 Use the words to write questions (?) and affirmative (+) or negative (-) sentences.
1 she / sing (+)
2 he / play the guitar (-)
3 she / speak Chinese (?)
4 he / swim (+)
5 they / spell (-)
6 you / dance (?)

5 💬 Work in pairs. Ask and answer questions about the activities in exercise 4. How many of your answers are the same?

> Can you sing?
>
> No, I can't.

6 💬 Work in pairs. Test yourself!

What can you do in English? — Test

Score ONE point for each thing you can do.

1 name six **colours**
2 write the names of ten animals
3 see three things that begin with the letter '**C**'
4 count backwards from 20 to 1 (**20**, **19**, **18**, …)
5 spell your teacher's name
6 say the days of the week

Starter

What's in this book?

1 Look through the Student's Book and answer the questions.
1. Each unit has a **Quick review** page. Where?
2. How many **Projects** are there in the book?
3. Where is the **Irregular verbs** list?
4. Where is the **Graphic organiser**?

2 There are lots of things to help you in the book. Find the answers to the questions.
1. In **WDYT? (What Do You Think?)** you think about a big question at the start of the unit, and again at the end. Lots of things in the unit help you think about the topic. What's the question in Unit 2?
2. In **Research** boxes you go online to find out more about a topic. What information do you research in Unit 4?
3. In **Video skills** you learn to think critically about videos. What's the first question in Video skills in Unit 6?
4. In **Reading subskills** you learn how to be a more effective reader. What's the subskill in Unit 1?
5. In **Word work** you meet new vocabulary in context in the reading texts. What's the first word you study in Unit 7?
6. In **Critical thinking** you learn to think more carefully about ideas in a text. What's question number 3 in the Critical thinking activity in Unit 5?
7. In **Listening subskills** you learn how to be a more effective listener. What's the subskill in Unit 3?
8. In **Super skills** you practise things which are important in everyday life. What Super skill do you practise in the Project in Unit 8?

3 In which unit do you see photos 1–8?

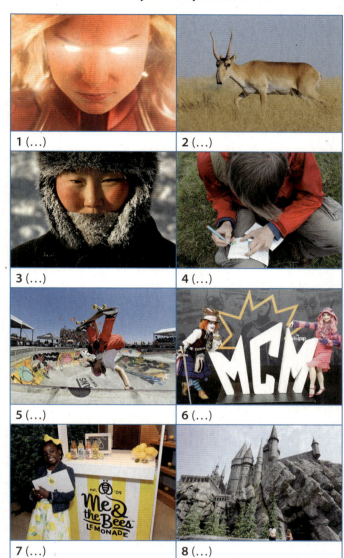

1 (...) 2 (...)
3 (...) 4 (...)
5 (...) 6 (...)
7 (...) 8 (...)

4 Work in pairs. Complete the challenge.

Classroom CHALLENGE

1. In which unit do you plan an ideal school timetable?
2. In which unit do you learn to describe animals?
3. In which unit do you listen to a hockey player?
4. Where do you 'Think – Prepare – Practise – Perform' in every unit?
5. In which unit do you visit Comic Con?
6. What are the four steps in the final Writing activity?

How quickly can you find the answers?

7. In which unit do you study modal verbs of obligation?
8. In which unit do you talk about holidays?
9. In which unit do you give a presentation on a hero?
10. Where do you learn Super skills?
11. In which Project do you make a mini-book?
12. In which unit do you study food vocabulary?

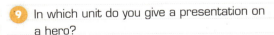

1 School life

(What do you think?)

What is an ideal school?

At my school in France, we have two hours for lunch. Some students **1** (…) home, but others **2** (…) lunch in the school canteen. There are no packed lunches!

I'm from Ghana and in my family we **6** (…) at four o'clock in the morning. I often help at home before I **7** (…) to school. I walk 6 km to and from school because there isn't a bus.

In Brazil, some students **4** (…) school at seven o'clock in the morning and **5** (…) at 12 o'clock. My school is different. We study from 12 o'clock until five in the afternoon.

Vocabulary: daily routines; school subjects

Grammar: present simple; object pronouns

Reading: an online article about online schools

Listening: a conversation with a Finnish student

Speaking: working together to check answers

Writing: a blog post

Project: design a timetable for your ideal school

Video skills p13

Real-world speaking p19

Project pp22–23

Daily routines

1  When do students usually do the activities in the box? Copy and complete the table.

| do homework finish school get up go home go to bed go to school have breakfast have dinner have lunch start school |

Morning	Afternoon	Evening
		do homework

2 Complete the facts on the map with words from exercise 1.

3 Work in pairs. What things are similar and different in your school day?

Vocabulary 1

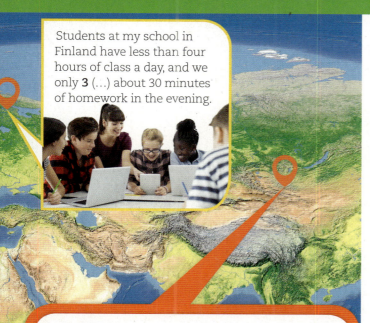

Students at my school in Finland have less than four hours of class a day, and we only **3** (...) about 30 minutes of homework in the evening.

My typical day

1. On schooldays, I **wake up** at quarter past six, and get up five minutes later. I **have a shower** and **brush my hair**.

2. I have breakfast – noodles or porridge – at about quarter to seven. I **clean my teeth** and then I go to school with my friends.

3. I **get dressed** in my school uniform and I **pack my bag** for school. I usually **make my bed** and **tidy my room**, but sometimes I forget!

4. We start school at half past seven and **have a break** at ten to ten. We all do physical exercises together.

5. We have lunch at half past twelve and finish school at four o'clock. I go home and **get changed** into my normal clothes.

6. I have dinner with my family at about half past five, and then I do homework for about three hours. I go to bed at ten o'clock and **go to sleep** – I'm usually really tired!

4 Read about a Chinese student's typical day. Match paragraphs 1–6 with pictures A–F.

5 Match the times with the activities from a Chinese student's typical day.

6 Put the activities in the order you do them on a typical day.

1. make my bed / wake up / get up
2. brush my hair / get dressed / have a shower
3. have breakfast / make my bed / clean my teeth
4. have a break / pack my bag / start school
5. go to sleep / go to bed / clean my teeth

> **Time and day**
>
> Use *at* with times – *at half past six, at ten o'clock*
> Use *in* with parts of the day – *in the morning, in the afternoon, in the evening* BUT *at night*
> Use *on* with days – *on Monday(s), on Tuesday(s)*

7 Complete the sentences with *at*, *in* or *on*.

1. We finish school early (...) Fridays.
2. I sometimes have a shower (...) the evening.
3. I usually have breakfast (...) about seven o'clock.
4. I clean my teeth (...) the morning and (...) night.
5. My first class (...) Monday morning is maths.

8 Work in pairs. Tell your partner about your typical day. What is the same and what is different?

9 Watch the video. What daily activities do you see students do?

10 Work in pairs. Discuss the questions.

1. Why did the vlogger make the video?
2. Who do you think this video is for?
3. How does the vlogger make the video interesting? Think about: how long you see each image, the music, her voice, etc.

1 Reading and critical thinking

An online article

1 Match the words in the box with pictures A–J.

> get dressed   get up   go home   go to school
> go to sleep   have a break   have lunch
> pack my bag   start school   wake up

2 Order the activities of a typical school day in exercise 1. Add three more activities to the list.

▶ **Subskill: Predicting from the title and the pictures**

Look at photos and the title of a text <u>before you read</u>. This can help you understand what is in the text.

3 Look at the pictures on p15 and read the title of the article. Answer the questions.
1 What day and time is it in the pictures?
2 Why are the students at home?
3 What daily routine activities do you think the students do? What don't they do?

4 🔊 7 Read and listen to the article. What daily routine activities do the students do?

5 Read the article again. Are the sentences true or false? Correct the false sentences.
1 An online school has lessons at fixed times.
2 Students see the whiteboard on their computer.
3 They can communicate with the teacher.
4 Students work on the computer all day.
5 They see their classmates outside school.
6 Online students study different subjects from students in other schools.

6 Complete the sentences.
1 Jack starts school at …
2 Abi has her first lesson at …
3 In the morning, they have …
4 They have lunch, and then they …
5 Jack learns about …
6 They see friends in …

7 **Word work** Match the definitions to the words in bold in the text.
1 numbers or letters that show how good schoolwork is
2 things you learn at school, e.g. maths or English
3 a place where you can borrow or read books
4 start to use a computer
5 students in your class
6 visits with other students

8 Complete the sentences with words from exercise 7.
1 We sometimes go on (…) to museums or other places of interest.
2 There's a big (…) at my school with lots of books.
3 Our teacher gives us (…) from one to ten for our homework.
4 The first thing we in do in computer classes is (…).
5 I often walk to school with one of my (…).
6 We have science (…) every Friday morning.

CRITICAL THINKING

1 **Understand** Think about online and traditional schools. Find at least two things that are the same and two things that are different.
2 **Evaluate** Which of these things is an advantage of an online school? Which is a disadvantage?
3 **Create** Think of three advantages of a traditional school.

Learning ZONE

Online learning | My story | News | Events   Subscribe

A DAY IN THE LIFE OF AN ONLINE STUDENT

Every year, more and more teens study at online high schools. They don't go to school like other students. They stay at home and connect to classes via the Internet. So, what is a typical day for an online student?

The fact is, it depends. Students have lessons, but they can study when they want. Jack wakes up at seven and reads for an hour before breakfast. He starts his lessons at nine. Abi prefers to start school early, so she has free time for sports and other activities in the afternoon.

'I get up and **log on** for my first lesson at eight' she says. 'I read the notes on the whiteboard on my computer.' Abi doesn't see her teachers, but she can hear them. Later, she can ask questions online or by phone.

Both Jack and Abi have four lessons in the morning. After lunch, they do homework and class projects. 'I don't sit at the computer all day,' says Jack. 'I make robots, or I go to the **library** and learn about the things I like.'

Of course, online students don't see their **classmates** every day. They sometimes go on **school trips** together, but they only meet friends in after-school clubs. They also need to be motivated, because they spend a lot of time studying alone.

In other ways, online schools are the same as ordinary schools. 'We do all the normal **subjects** like maths and history,' says Abi. 'We do tests and we get **grades** for our work.'

Click here to find out what other students say about online learning.

The longer read → Resource centre

1 Grammar

Present simple: affirmative and negative

1 Read the examples. Copy and complete the table with the verbs in blue.

> I *get up* at eight.
> They *don't go* to school. They *stay* at home.
> Jack *wakes up* at seven.
> Abi *doesn't see* her teachers.
> I *don't sit* at the computer all day.

Affirmative		
I/You	*get up*	at eight.
He/She/It	1 (…)	at seven.
We/They	2 (…)	at home.
Negative		
I/You	3 (…)	at the computer all day.
He/She/It	4 (…)	her teachers.
We/They	*don't go*	to school.

2 Choose the correct option.
1. We **don't go/doesn't go** to school on Saturdays.
2. Many students **start/starts** school before nine o'clock.
3. My younger brother **don't study/doesn't study** at weekends.
4. Our school **open/opens** at half past eight.
5. I **don't do/doesn't do** homework in the morning.
6. Our school year **start/starts** in September.

3 Read the Spelling rules on p21. Write the third person singular of the verbs in the box.

> finish   get up   go   have
> make   play   study   watch

4 Complete the sentences with the present simple of the verbs in brackets.
1. I (…) **(wake up)** at seven o'clock but I (…) **(not get up)** until a quarter past.
2. My brother (…) **(not make)** his bed on schooldays. My dad (…) **(make)** it.
3. I (…) **(have)** cereal for breakfast but my mum (…) **(have)** toast.
4. My sister (…) **(go)** to school before me.
5. Our teacher (…) **(give)** us homework, but we (…) **(not get)** much at weekends.
6. My brother (…) **(study)** for six hours every weekend.

5 Change the underlined words to make the sentences true for you.
1. I go to <u>an online school</u>.
   I don't go to an online school. I go to a …
2. My school day starts at <u>11 o'clock</u>.
3. We have a break at <u>half past nine</u>.
4. I study English on <u>Sundays</u>.
5. My school day finishes at <u>six o'clock</u>.
6. <u>My parents</u> do my homework.

6 🔊 8 Complete the text with the correct form of the verbs. Then listen and check.

Can you imagine going to a school like HOGWARTS?

In many ways, Hogwarts, in the Harry Potter books, is a normal boarding school. A typical day 1 (…) **(start)** with breakfast in the Great Hall. Then a bell 2 (…) **(ring)** and the students go to class. They 3 (…) **(have)** two classes before lunch, and two more classes in the afternoon. They even 4 (…) **(do)** homework and exams, and they get grades for their work.

But students 5 (…) **(not study)** normal subjects, they learn about magic. And Harry 6 (…) **(not play)** football, he plays quidditch.

You probably think that schools like Hogwarts 7 (…) **(not exist)**, but there is a real-life wizardry school in California. It 8 (…) **(teach)** students all about magic!

7 Answer the question to solve the Brain teaser.

	School start time			Likes		
	8:00 am	8:45 am	9:15 am	chess	music	dance
Tom						
Ana						
Sara						

1. Tom starts school before Ana.
2. Sara likes dance. She is the first to start school in the morning.
3. Ana doesn't like chess.

What do you know about Tom, Ana and Sara? (Clue: each answer is true for only <u>one</u> student.)

Vocabulary and Listening 1

School subjects

1 Look at the extract from a British school timetable and find …
1 two sciences
2 one creative subject
3 one foreign language

Class B	MONDAY	TUESDAY	WEDNESDAY
9:30–10:10	maths	English literature	chemistry
10:10–10:50	history	French	maths
10:50–11:10	BREAK		
11:10–11:50	biology	ICT	ICT
11:50–12:30	PE	maths	PE
12:30–1:10	LUNCH BREAK		
1:10–2:00	basketball practice		
2:00–2:40	design and technology	music	geography
2:40–3:20	English language	music	citizenship
Homework	maths English biology	French maths	chemistry maths geography

2 Add the following subjects to groups 1–3 in exercise 1.

art   drama   German   physics

3 🔊 9 Listen to extracts 1–6 and match each one to a subject from the timetable.

4 💬 Work in pairs. Tell your partner which is your favourite day on the timetable and why.

> Which is your favourite day?

> Tuesday, because I like French and they've got double music.

A conversation

Hi! I'm Ansa. I'm from Hamina in Finland but this month I'm in York, England, visiting family and going to a British school.

▶ **Subskill: Identifying the type of listening**

To identify the type of listening, think about: people (how many?), places (where are they?) and language (is it formal or informal?).

5 🔊 10 Listen and choose the correct description.
a An interview with Ansa on local radio
b Ansa talking to a teacher
c A dialogue between Ansa and a classmate

6 Listen again. Which sentences are true?
1 Ansa thinks school in Britain is similar to her school.
2 Ansa starts school at half past eight.
3 Ansa has school after lunch.
4 Ansa doesn't have any exams.
5 In a project, all the students work on the same thing.
6 Finnish students study subjects in separate lessons.

7 Correct the false sentences in exercise 6.

8 💬 Work in pairs. Would you like to go to Ansa's school? Why/Why not? Tell your partner.

> I'd like to go to Ansa's school because I'd like to do projects.

> Really? I prefer to study separate subjects.

 fun facts In Finland, students start school when they're seven years old.

Pronunciation: Silent letters → p116

1 Grammar

Present simple: Yes/No questions

1 Read the examples. Copy and complete the table.

Do you have history lessons in school?	Yes, we do.
Does your school start later?	No, it doesn't.
Do you go back in the afternoon?	No, I don't.

Yes/No questions and short answers		
Do		think it's different?
Yes,	I / **1** (…) /we/they	**2** (…).
No,		don't.
3 (…)		start at eight o'clock?
4 (…),	he/she/it	does.
No,		**5** (…).

2 Match the questions with the short answers in the box.

| Yes, she does.   Yes, I do.   Yes, we do. |
| No, it doesn't.   No, they don't. |

1 Does your school have a swimming pool?
2 Do you and your classmates study French?
3 Do the students wear a uniform?
4 Does your teacher use a computer?
5 Do you like your school?

3 Write questions. Use *Do* or *Does*.

1 you / start school / eight o'clock ?
  Do you start school at eight o'clock?
2 your class / study / German ?
3 you / have lessons / Saturdays ?
4 your school / finish / 3:30 ?
5 your teachers / give / homework ?

4 💬 Work in pairs. Take turns to ask the questions and answer with short answers.

Object pronouns

| We present **them**. |
| I can't imagine studying **it**. |

5 Copy and complete the table with the object pronouns in the box.

| her   him   it   me   us   you |

Subject	I	you	he	she	it	we	they
Object	**1** (…)	**2** (…)	**3** (…)	**4** (…)	**5** (…)	**6** (…)	them

6 Replace the words in bold with an object pronoun.

1 **PE** is my favourite sport – I love **PE**!
2 Our art teacher, Mr Flynn, is great – we like **Mr Flynn** a lot.
3 I think science subjects are really difficult. I don't like **science subjects**.
4 I go to school with Sara and I come home with **Sara** too.
5 Our maths teacher always gives **our class** lots of homework.

7 Choose the correct option.

GRAMMAR ROUND-UP
1 2 3 4 5 6 7 8

Teach yourself!

If you **1** want/wants to learn something new, why not use your phone? You **2** can download/can to download lots of great learning apps and use **3** they/them to learn all kinds of things, from languages to computer coding.

Are you into video? *Magisto* and *Openshot* are great apps to learn video editing. If **4** you no know/you don't know how to do your design and technology homework, then *Instructables* is the app for you. *WikiHow* is a great option too! And if you **5** want/do want help with art, go for *MyPaint* or *Krita*. It **6** do has/has some fantastic ideas to help you.

7 Do they cost/Cost they a lot of money? **8** No, they don't cost./No, they don't. Most of the apps are free.

Research

Find one of the apps in the article online. Would it be useful for you?

Real-world speaking

Working together to check answers

1 Look at four things students do in class. In which activities do you work together?
- a playing a game
- b doing an exam
- c checking answers to an exercise
- d asking what the homework is

2 🎥 Watch the video. What is the activity? Choose from a–d in exercise 1.

3 Watch again. Which Key phrases do you hear?

4 Complete the dialogue with the Key phrases. Watch again and check.

Carmel: What **1** (…) number 1? I've got 'Australia'.
Lukas: Yes, me too. OK – what about number 2? I've **2** (…) 'Sydney'.
Carmel: Are you sure? I've got 'Canberra'. Let's leave that one.
Lukas: OK, and number 3? The number of states …
Carmel: I don't **3** (…) .
Lukas: I think it's 'six'.
Carmel: OK, six. Now, number 4. I **4** (…) it's '34 million'.
Lukas: Are you **5** (…) ? I've got '24 million'.
Carmel: Oops, yes, you're right. I can't read my writing!
Lukas: Right. Number 5 – the national sport. Do **6** (…) think it's 'rugby'?
Carmel: Let's see … 'rugby'! High five!

5 Create your own dialogue. Follow the steps in the Skills boost.

SKILLS BOOST

THINK
Work individually. You have five minutes to complete the Geography quiz below.

PREPARE
In pairs, use your answers to the quiz to prepare a dialogue of students checking together. Remember to use the Key phrases for working together.

PRACTISE
Practise your dialogue.

PERFORM
Act out your dialogue for the class.

Geography quiz
1. Which city is not in Canada: Montreal, Seattle or Toronto?
2. Is the Antarctic in the north or the south?
3. What's the next planet: Mercury, Venus, Earth, … ?
4. Which is the capital of Turkey: Ankara or Istanbul?
5. In which continent is Mount Kilimanjaro?

6 **Peer review** Listen to your classmates and answer the questions.
1. Which Key phrases do they use?
2. Do you agree with their answers to the quiz?

Key phrases
Asking about a question: What about number … ?
What have you got for number … ?
Do you think it's … ?
Giving your answer: I've got …
I think it's …
Agreeing on the same answer: Yes, me too.
You're right.
Disagreeing (you have a different answer):
Really? I've got …
Are you sure?
Saying you don't know the answer: I don't know.

Real-world grammar
I think it's '34 million'.
Do you think it's 'rugby'?

Phrasebook → p122

Writing

Tell us about your school

1. How many students are in your school?
2. Have you got a uniform?
3. How many teachers are in the school?
4. What subjects do you study?
5. Do you use computers?
6. What time does school start and when does it finish?
7. Do you have lunch at school?
8. What sports do you do?
9. What are your favourite things about school?

Questions by English Class A, Kyoto High School, Japan

All About My School

Our high school is in the centre of Tirana, Albania. It's a big school, with about 900 students. The teachers are OK – they aren't too strict. We haven't got a school uniform.

My favourite subjects are PE and ICT. We also study maths, biology, chemistry, English history and Albanian. I love computers but we don't use them a lot at my school.

We start school at 7:30 in the morning – it's too early! But we finish at two o'clock and I have lunch at home. In the afternoon, I relax for a bit and then I do my homework. I normally have about three hours of homework every day. In the evening, I play video games or go out to play basketball with my friends.

posted by Altin at 14:59

A blog post

All About My School is an international project where teachers and students from different countries post descriptions about school life where they live and answer questions from students in other countries.

1 Read the questions and answers in the blog. Does the writer answer all the questions?

2 Read the blog post again and find the answers to questions 1–9 in Altin's answer.

3 Match headings a–c with each paragraph in the blog.
- a Subjects
- b School day and free time
- c General description of the school, the students and teachers

4 Is Altin's school life similar or different to yours? Why?

▶ **Subskill: Capital letters**

In English, some words have a capital letter. Remember that it isn't just the first word at the start of a sentence, e.g. *I have a French class on Monday.*

5 Read the school subjects. Find two rules for using capital letters.

art	English	French	geography
ICT	maths	PE	

6 Read the list. When do we use a capital letter in English?
- a for I, e.g. *Can I use your pen?* ✓
- b at the start of a sentence
- c for all nouns
- d for days of the week
- e for greetings
- f for months of the year
- g for names and surnames
- h for people's titles
- i for cities, countries and nationalities

7 💬 Work in pairs. Read Altin's description and explain the reason for each capital letter.

8 Correct the text, adding capital letters where necessary.

> ~~hi!~~ Hi i'm pearl. i live in edinburgh, in scotland. the school year here starts in august and finishes in june. we have classes five days a week, from monday to friday. my favourite subjects are pe and german. all our teachers are very nice but my favourite is our biology teacher, mr liddle.

9 Write an entry about your school life for the *All About My School* blog. Follow the steps in the Skills boost.

SKILLS BOOST

THINK
Write your answers to the questions in *All About My School*.

PREPARE
Organise the information from your answers into three paragraphs. Use the paragraph headings and order from exercise 3.
Paragraph 1:
Paragraph 2:
Paragraph 3:

WRITE
Write your blog post. Use Altin's post to help you.

CHECK
Answer the questions.
1 Is the blog post interesting to read?
2 Do you use paragraphs?
3 Do you use the present simple correctly?
4 Do you use capital letters correctly?

10 **Peer review** Exchange your blog post with another student. Answer the questions.
1 Does the writer use the present simple and capital letters correctly?
2 Does the post give clear information about school life in your country?
3 Do you know anything new about your classmate now?

QUICK REVIEW 1

Grammar

Present simple
Affirmative
With *he/she/it* the verb ends in *-s*, *-es* or *-ies*.
I **get up** at seven o'clock.   She **goes** to sleep at 10:30.

Negative
I/you/we/they: subject + *don't* + verb
he/she/it: subject + *doesn't* + verb
We **don't have** a school uniform.   He **doesn't study** French.

Yes/No questions and short answers
Do + *I/you/we/they* + verb?   Yes, I/you/we/they do.
                                    No, I/you/we/they don't.
Does + *he/she/it* + verb?   Yes, he/she/it does.
                                    No, he/she/it doesn't.

Do they **study** music?   Yes, they **do**.
Does the school **have** a gym? No, it **doesn't**.

Spelling rules for *he/she/it*
For most verbs, add -s:
read → he read**s**   wake up → she wake**s** up
For verbs that end in -s, -sh, -ss, -ch, -x or -o, add -es:
go → it go**es**   teach → she teach**es**   mix → he mix**es**
For verbs that end in consonant + y, omit the y and add -ies:
study → he stud**ies**
Some verbs are irregular: have → she **has**

Subject and object pronouns
Subject pronouns: I, you, he, she, it, we, they
Object pronouns: me, you, him, her, it, us, them
I start my homework at six o'clock and finish **it** at seven.
Can **you** help **us**?

Vocabulary

🔊 11 **Daily routines**
brush my hair, clean my teeth, do homework, finish school, get changed, get dressed, get up, go home, go to bed, go to school, go to sleep, have a break, have a shower, have breakfast, have dinner, have lunch, make my bed, pack my bag, tidy my room, start school, wake up

🔊 12 **School subjects**
art, biology, chemistry, citizenship, design and technology, drama, English language, English literature, French, geography, German, history, ICT, maths, music, PE, physics

21

Project

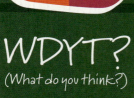

WDYT? (What do you think?)

What is an ideal school?

TASK: Design a timetable for your ideal school.

Learning outcomes
1. I can talk about the importance of different school subjects.
2. I can make logical decisions.
3. I can use appropriate language from the unit.

Graphic organiser ➡ Project planner p118

1 🎥 Watch a video of students talking about their ideal timetable. What school subjects do they mention?

STEP 1: THINK ▪▫▫▫

2 Look at the photos and the timetable in the Model project. What school subjects can you see in the photos?

3 What do you learn in these subjects? Match 1–4 with a–d.
1. money management
2. cyber-security
3. public speaking
4. inventing

a. how to speak to a group of people
b. how to be safe online
c. how to create new things
d. how to use money

4 Are the school subjects useful? Why/Why not?

STEP 2: PLAN ▪▪▫▫

5 Work in pairs. Read the tips in the Super skills box and practise saying the Key phrases with a partner.

CRITICAL THINKING

Making logical decisions

Tips
Don't make a quick decision.
List the advantages and disadvantages.
Think about the advantages and disadvantages before you decide.

Key phrases
Wait a moment. Yes, but don't forget …
Slow down. I'd like to learn …
What about … ? Me too.
I think/don't think that's a good thing.
Really? I'd prefer …

6 Work in pairs. Make notes about your ideal school timetable. Use the tips and Key phrases in the Super skills box.
- the time of the school day – when it starts and finishes
- the number of minutes for each lesson
- the school subjects that you want to study

STEP 3: CREATE ▪▪▪▫

7 In your notebook, prepare a timetable for a week of classes.

8 Write sentences about your school timetable. Explain your decisions.

Our school day starts at … and finishes at … because …
Our first lesson is …
We think it's …
Students learn music because we think …

Grammar and Vocabulary ➡ Quick review p21

Model project

	MONDAY	TUESDAY	WEDNESDAY
9:00–9:50	yoga	app design	martial arts
9:50–10:40	Chinese	science	maths
10:40–11:00	BREAK		
11:00–11:50	chemistry	inventing	money management
11:50–12:40	history	English	cyber-security
12:40–13:30	film making	cookery	public speaking
13:30	LUNCH/GO HOME		

STEP 4: PRESENT

9 Read the *How to …* tips on p118. Then work with another pair. Tell them about your school timetable.

10 **Peer review** Choose the timetable you think is most interesting and useful for all students.

1 FINAL REFLECTION

1 The task
How well can you describe your ideal school timetable?
Can you explain your decisions? Give examples.

2 Super skill
Are your decisions logical? Say why.

3 Language
Do you use language from the unit? Give examples.

Me time

How important are hobbies for teenagers?

I take photos.

I play football.

Vocabulary: free-time activities; collocations with *do*, *go* and *play*

Grammar: adverbs of frequency; likes and dislikes; present simple *Wh-* questions

Reading: a blog about a champion skateboarder

Listening: a radio interview with a hockey player

Speaking: asking for information

Writing: informal messages

Project: do a survey about how students spend their free time

Video skills p25

Real-world speaking p31

Project pp34–35

Free-time activities

1 Work in pairs. Read the statistics. Does any of the information surprise you?

> I'm surprised American teenagers sleep for nearly 11 hours.

> Really? I'm not that surprised. I think …

2 Copy and complete the table with the free-time activities in red.

Media and communication	Sports	Art and music	Other

24

Vocabulary 2

I watch TV series.

FREE time in the USA
how teenagers spend their weekends

4.3 hours a day on media
Teens **sleep** for **10.9** hours a day
3.8 hours on hobbies
Teens spend **0.9** hours a day on sports
1.1 hours a day on schoolwork
Teens also **meet friends**, work and **listen to music**

© US bureau of Labor Statistic

We play video games.

3 Which free-time activities in the box do you see in photos 1–6? Add them all to the table in exercise 2.

> collect things   draw   go to a dance class
> go to the gym   help at home   make videos
> play chess   play in a band   play in a team
> practise the piano   use social media

4 Complete the description with words and phrases from exercise 3. Change the form of the verb if necessary.

> My brother Archie and I are twins but we're very different. I'm really into sport. I love football and I **1** (…) called the Midland Juniors. I have to be quick and strong for football, so I also **2** (…) once a week.
>
> Archie is very musical. He plays the guitar and he sometimes **3** (…) for three hours a day. At weekends, he **4** (…) with two friends.
>
> We both **5** (…) on our phones to chat to our friends and sometimes we **6** (…) to put on YouTube.
>
> But it isn't all fun! At weekends we also do homework and **7** (…).

5 How many hours do you spend on free-time activities at the weekend?

social media – 2 hours   *football – 1 hour*

6 Work in pairs. Talk about your free-time activities using your notes in exercise 5.

VIDEO SKILLS

7 Watch the video. What activities does the vlogger do at the weekend?

8 Work in pairs. Discuss the questions.
1 Which elements of the video help you to understand it? Think about:
  - images
  - text
  - the presenter
2 Why are vloggers popular?
3 Would you like to be a vlogger? Why/Why not?

2 Reading and critical thinking

A blog

1 🔊 13 Listen to people doing seven different free-time activities. Which activities do you hear?

2 Look at the photos on p27. Which of the things in the box can you see?

> ball girl graffiti hat people watching
> skateboard swimming pool table

3 Look at the text, but don't read it. Answer the question and explain your answer.

What type of text is this?
- a a newspaper article
- b part of a novel
- c a blog post

4 🔊 14 Read and listen to the text and choose the best summary.
- a Brighton's got lots of hobbies.
- b Brighton is a normal girl with a special talent.
- c Brighton's got a busy life.

▶ **Subskill: Reading for specific information**

To find specific information in a text, first identify key words in the exercise that will help you.

5 Read the text again and complete the sentences.
1. Brighton is (…) years old.
2. She studies in (…) grade.
3. One of her favourite musicians is (…) .
4. She likes watching videos on (…) .
5. She's extremely good at (…) .
6. She practises before and (…) school every day.
7. She feels (…) before competitions.

6 Match 1–5 to a–e to make sentences.

1	At home, Brighton does	a	sport at the Olympics.
2	Brighton is only 13, but	b	some things about being famous.
3	Skateboarding is a new	c	she's a champion in adult competitions.
4	Brighton doesn't like	d	she's a normal teenager too.
5	Brighton is famous but	e	the same things as other teenagers.

7 **Word work** Match the definitions to the words in bold in the text.
1. a very famous actor, singer or sports player
2. practises (a sport) seriously
3. fantastic, surprising
4. (in sport) for young people, not adults
5. a person who wins a competition
6. excited and worried at the same time

8 💬 Work in pairs. Ask and answer the questions.

Do you know anyone who … ?
- trains regularly with a football or basketball team
- gets nervous before doing something
- can take amazing photos
- is a champion swimmer

CRITICAL THINKING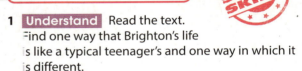

1. **Understand** Read the text. Find one way that Brighton's life is like a typical teenager's and one way in which it is different.

2. **Evaluate** If you become very good at a hobby, lots of things can change. Add some more advantages and disadvantages.

   Advantages
   You can meet people from other cities or countries.
   You can train and improve your technique.

   Disadvantages
   It's expensive.
   Your hobby stops being fun.

3. **Create** Imagine you can meet Brighton. Write three questions to ask her.

   Work in groups of four. Decide who is student A, B, C and D.

   Students A, B and C: Ask your questions.

   Student D: You are Brighton. Use your imagination and answer the questions!

Research

What other sports are in the X-Games? Find out more about one of them and present it to the class.

At the top of her game

6th October

THIS WEEK'S TALENTED TEEN IS BRIGHTON ZEUNER.

Brighton is 13. Like any other 8th grade student in the USA, in the evenings she usually does homework or listens to music in her bedroom. She likes Beyoncé. She hardly ever has free time but she loves watching videos on YouTube.

But Brighton, from Encinitas, California, is also an X-Games **champion** skateboarder. And not in a **junior** competition. No – Brighton is the world champion and competes against women twice her age. **Amazing**, right?

But the future looks even more exciting for Brighton. The big news is that skateboarding is now an Olympic sport! To prepare for the next X-Games and the Olympics, Brighton **trains** every morning before school, and in the afternoon she always practises in her local skate park.

Is it difficult to be famous when you're so young? Brighton says she is sometimes **nervous** when she gives interviews or before competitions, but it's all part of doing the sport she loves. And the great thing about Brighton is that she's a skateboarding **superstar**, but she's also a normal person like you or me.

♥ Like   💬 Reply

6th October | 7:45 pm
That's so cool! What an amazing example.
Suzy Skater

6th October | 8:10 pm
Let's hope Brighton gets the gold at the Olympics!
MarioBlogs

6th October | 10:13 pm
It's great that Brighton can still have a normal life.
Princess Carrie

Leave a comment
Enter your comment here:

NEWS

PHOTOS

ABOUT

EVENTS

FORUM

The longer read → Resource centre

2 Grammar

Adverbs of frequency

1 Read the examples. Copy and complete the table with the adverbs of frequency.

> In the evenings she usually does homework or listens to music.
> She always practises in her local skate park.
> She is sometimes nervous when she gives interviews.
> She hardly ever has free time.

More frequent					Less frequent
1 (…)	2 (…)	often	3 (…)	4 (…)	never

2 Read the sentences in exercise 1 again and choose the correct option to complete the rules.
1 With the verb *be*, the adverb comes **before/after** the verb.
2 With other verbs, the adverb comes **before/after** the verb.

3 Rewrite the sentences with the adverbs of frequency in the correct position.
1 I am late home on Mondays. (**always**)
   I am always late home on Mondays.
2 Frankie practises the piano for hours. (**often**)
3 Ahmed does his homework before playing video games. (**usually**)
4 They are very tired after going to their dance class. (**sometimes**)
5 My sister takes lots of photos when we go on holiday. (**always**)
6 Lily helps her parents at home. (**hardly ever**)
7 My best friend is hungry after baseball practice. (**always**)

Likes and dislikes

4 Copy and complete the table with the verbs in the box.

| don't like   don't mind   hate   love |

😍	🙂	😐	😫	😡
1 (…)	like	2 (…)	3 (…)	4 (…)

5 Read the examples. Copy and complete the table with the words in the box.

> She likes Beyoncé.
> I love watching videos.
> He doesn't mind practising the piano.

| doesn't mind   love   she   verb -*ing*   we |

Subject	Verb	Noun, 3 (…)
I/you/ 1 (…) / they	2 (…) /like/don't mind/don't like/hate	tennis. sleeping.
he/ 4 (…) /it	loves/likes/ 5 (…) / doesn't like/hates	

6 Read the information and write sentences.
1 They 😡 play / chess.
2 She 😍 draw / manga comics.
3 I 🙂 Barcelona.
4 We 😐 help / our parents.
5 He 😫 play / video games.

7 Complete the text with the correct form of the words in brackets.

> American teenager Carissa Yip is an international chess champion – a grandmaster. She **1** (…) (**play / often**) in adult competitions and the adults **2** (…) (**be / sometimes**) angry when she wins. She **3** (…) (**lose / hardly ever**). Carissa **4** (…) (**love / play**) chess but she also likes other things: she **5** (…) (**like / sushi**) and she **6** (…) (**love / play**) with her grandmother's cat when she visits China. Carissa also **7** (…) (**like / make**) videos and she **8** (…) (**post / often**) comments and videos on websites for chess fans.

8 Answer the question to solve the Brain teaser.

> Jimmy and Jenny have lots of hobbies. They like swimming and they both like collecting things. They don't like sport or drawing. Jimmy loves sleeping and Jenny likes chess.
>
> *Do they like taking photos?*
> *(Clue: think about the letters in the words!)*

Collocations with *do, go* and *play*

1 Read the advert. Is the sports centre a good place for these people?

1 I enjoy team sports.
2 I only like winter sports.
3 I want to do **martial arts**.
4 I like playing ball games.
5 I prefer water sports.
6 I love dancing.

LIVE WELL Sports Centre

- Do you want to keep fit, meet people and have fun?
- We have all kinds of activities. Check out our timetables and clubs.
- A great place to go **swimming**!
- Play **hockey** – learn team spirit!
- Do **aerobics** with our expert instructors!

NEWS
- Our sports hall is now open again for **basketball** and **volleyball**.
- We now offer **hip hop** classes every Monday and Saturday.
- Join our **roller-skating** disco every Saturday!

Hockey
Karate
Aerobics
Saturday night roller-skating disco

2 What sports can each person from exercise 1 do at the sports centre?

3 Read the advert again. Complete the rules with *do, go* and *play*.
1 We use (…) with ball sports.
2 We use (…) with verb *-ing*.
3 We use (…) with other activities.

Vocabulary and Listening 2

4 Copy and complete the table with the activities from the advert. Then add the sports in the box.

athletics   badminton   cycling   gymnastics
horse-riding   skateboarding   skiing   surfing
table tennis   yoga

Do	Go	Play
karate		

5 Work in pairs. Ask and answer questions about the activities in exercise 4.

Do you play basketball?
Yes, I do. What about you?
No, I don't, but I like watching it.

A radio interview

Subskill: Listening for the general idea
When you listen for general understanding, wait until you finish listening before you choose your answer.

6 🔊 15 Listen to an interview with a hockey player. What does the player talk about?
a how sports help you to keep fit
b the rules of hockey
c the advantages of team sports

7 Listen again. Why does Ben think hockey is a good sport? Which ideas does he mention?
1 you learn to work in a team
2 you learn from mistakes
3 players help each other
4 it teaches you to work in groups
5 you learn to work hard
6 you learn to be organised

8 Listen again and answer the questions.
1 How old are the players in the hockey team?
2 How many players are in Ben's team?
3 When do they practise?
4 What other sport does he do?

9 Work in pairs. Answer the questions.
1 What are the advantages of individual sports?
2 Which do you prefer, team sports or individual sports? Why?

2 Grammar

Present simple: Wh- questions

1 Copy the tables and add questions a–c.
  a Why do you like hockey?
  b When have you got your next match?
  c Who is the team captain?

be questions

Question word	am/is/are	subject	
Why	is	hockey	important to you?
How old	are	the players?	

have got questions

Question word	have/has	subject	got	
How many people	have	you	got	in your team?
Why	has	the team	got	16 players?

Questions with other present simple verbs

Question word	do/does	subject	verb	
How	does	hockey	help	you?
When	do	you	play?	

2 Order the words to make questions.
  1 you / have / PE / When / got ?
  2 favourite / are / What / your / sports ?
  3 keep fit / How / you / do ?
  4 does / play / Where / your local football team ?
  5 is / Who / your favourite sports star ?

3 💬 Work in pairs. Ask and answer the questions in exercise 2.

4 Complete the sports quiz questions with the correct words.

Do the sports quiz!

1 How (...) you say 40-40 in tennis?
  a equals   b deuce   c forty-forty
2 What (...) surfing, skateboarding and karate got in common?
  a They're adventure sports. b They come from Australia.
  c They're Olympic sports.
3 What (...) the name of the New Zealand rugby team?
  a All Whites   b All Blacks   c All Reds
4 When (...) the NBA basketball season usually begin?
  a September   b October   c November
5 How many rings (...) on the Olympic flag?
  a five   b six   c seven

5 🔊 16 Choose the correct answers in the quiz. Listen and check.

6 Write questions with *is, are, do, does* and *have got*.
  1 What / you / do in your free time ?
  2 When / you / do it ?
  3 How many video games / you ?
  4 What / your favourite game ?
  5 Why / you / like it ?

7 💬 Work in pairs. Ask and answer the questions in exercise 6.

8 Choose the correct option.

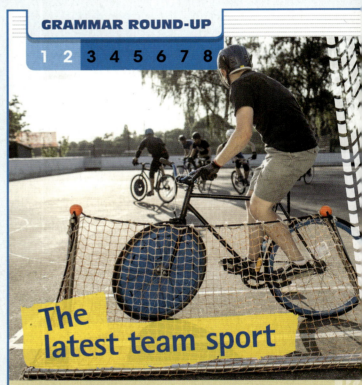

GRAMMAR ROUND-UP
1 2 **3 4 5 6 7 8**

The latest team sport

What game **1 do/does** you play with a hockey ball and a bicycle? The answer is simple: bike polo.

Bike polo is over 100 years old. It **2 come/comes** from Ireland, but now it's popular all over the world.

People **3 usually play/play usually** polo on horses, but in this sport all you need is a bike. It **4 doesn't cost/don't cost** a lot of money, and each team **5 has/have** only got three players.

Brendan Fox, aged 15, loves **6 play/playing** bike polo. You can see **7 he/him** on his bike every day after school. Why **8 does he like/he likes** it? 'Well, it **9 is sometimes/sometimes is** a bit dangerous,' he says, 'but it's really good fun.'

Pronunciation: *do you* /djʊ/ → p116

Real-world speaking 2

MONDAY
Let's cook! Street food
5:00–6:00 pm
Photography
6:00–7:30 pm

TUESDAY
Yoga
4:30–5:30 pm
Easy robotics
5:30–7:00 pm

WEDNESDAY
Painting for beginners
4:00–5:30 pm

THURSDAY
Movie-making
4:30–5:30 pm
Chess
5:00–6:00 pm

FRIDAY
Drawing masterclass
3:30–4:30 pm
Coding and app building
7:00–9:00 pm

LEARN SOMETHING new today!

Asking for information

1 Look at the leaflet. Which course would you like to do?

2 🎥 Watch the video. Which course does Maria choose?

3 Watch again. Which questions in the Key phrases box does Maria ask?

4 Complete the dialogue with the Key phrases. Watch again and check.

Maria: Excuse me. Hi. I'd like to **1** (…) your courses, please.
Receptionist: Oh, hello. Yes, of course.
Maria: **2** (…) a photography course?
Receptionist: Just one moment. Yes, we do. It's on Mondays, from 6 to 7:30.
Maria: That isn't good for me. I always play basketball on Mondays.
Receptionist: We have a painting class on Wednesdays.
Maria: I don't like painting. Thanks anyway.
Receptionist: What about movie-making? That's on Thursdays, from 4:30 to 5:30.
Maria: **3** (…) is it?
Receptionist: Let's see. It's $75 for ten classes, but the first class is free.
Maria: Great! Can I **4** (…) ?
Receptionist: Of course, just one moment …

5 Create your own dialogue. Follow the steps in the Skills boost.

SKILLS BOOST

THINK
Choose an activity from the leaflet, or think of another activity.

PREPARE
Prepare a dialogue. Use the information about days and times from the leaflet, or use your own ideas.

PRACTISE
Practise your dialogue. Take turns to ask for and give information.

PERFORM
Act out your dialogue for the class.

6 **Peer review** Listen to your classmates and answer the questions.
1 What activity do they choose?
2 What questions do they use to ask for information?

Key phrases
I'd like to find out about your courses, please.
Can you tell me about your photography course?
What time does it start?
How much is it?
Do you have a … course?
Can I sign up for it?
What day is it on?

 US → UK

Do you have a photography course? (US)
→ **Have you got** a photography course? (UK)

Phrasebook → p122

2 Writing

A Hi everyone!
My name's Akio and I'm from Japan. I'd love to have a pen pal. I like all kinds of sports. I do karate and I love watching baseball. Baseball is very popular in Japan. Do you like sports? Who is your favourite sports person? What sports are popular in your country? Hope to hear from you soon!

B CALLING ALL STUDENTS!
We want to find out what people do in their free time for a class project. We need your help!

How do you spend your free time? What are your hobbies and why do you like them?

Please write us a short note and send it to Nick and Ava.

Cheers!

C Hi Ed!
I'd like to find out about the Tech Club. I know you're a member. When does the club meet? Where do you have the club? What exactly do you do in it?
Let me know!
Ciara

Informal messages

1 Read the messages and answer the questions.
1 Who is each message to and from?
2 Why does each person write their message?

2 Read the reply. Which message does it answer?

Hi!

We meet on Thursdays after school at four. We usually finish at five, but we sometimes stay until half past five. We meet in the computer lab, but most people bring their own laptops or tablets. Alex from Class 5A organises the club and he's really great! He knows loads about coding. We do different things – it depends. We often work in groups. Some people create websites or blogs. Other people design apps. We all learn how to install software and solve problems with viruses.

Let me know if you want to go on Thursday. We can meet and go together.

See you soon!

3 Read the reply in exercise 2 again and answer the questions from the original message.

▶ **Subskill: *and*, *or* and *but***

We use *and*, *or* and *but* to connect ideas in a sentence.

4 Find examples of *and*, *or* and *but* in the reply in exercise 2. Complete the rules.

| and | or | but |

1 We use (…) to add a different idea.
2 We use (…) to add an alternative.
3 We use (…) to add a similar idea.

QUICK REVIEW 2

5 Complete the sentences with *and*, *or* and *but*.
1. On Saturday afternoons, I visit a friend. We go to her house (…) we meet in town.
2. I like doing sports, (…) I don't like watching them.
3. I like painting (…) I like drawing too.
4. I have a guitar lesson on Mondays (…) I go swimming on Thursdays.
5. Which do you prefer, football (…) basketball?
6. We sometimes go to the cinema, (…) it's very expensive.

6 Write a message. Answer message A or B in exercise 1. Follow the steps in the Skills boost.

SKILLS BOOST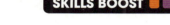

THINK
1. Choose message A or B.
2. What questions does the person ask?
3. What information do you need to give in your answer?

PREPARE
Make notes about your answers to the questions.
Question 1:
Question 2:
Question 3:

WRITE
Write your message.
Hi!/Hi Akio, …
I usually … in my free time.
I like … but I don't like …
Most people like …

CHECK
Read your message. Answer the questions.
1. Do you answer the three questions?
2. Do you use adverbs of frequency (*usually, always,* …)?
3. Do you use verb *-ing* after *like*, *love*, … ?
4. Do you use *and*, *or* and *but* correctly?

7 **Peer review** Exchange your message with another student. Answer the questions.
1. Does the writer use adverbs of frequency, verbs to express likes and dislikes, and *and*, *or* and *but* correctly?
2. Does the writer answer all the questions in the original message?

Grammar

Adverbs of frequency
always, usually, often, sometimes, hardly ever, never
be → adverb of frequency
We're **never** late for class.
I'm **sometimes** nervous before exams.
adverb of frequency → other verbs
We **usually** watch TV in the evenings.
My friends and I **always** go to the skate park at the weekend.
My brother **hardly ever** does sports.

Likes and dislikes
love, like, don't mind, don't like, hate

… + verb -ing	… + noun
I **love** skateboarding.	I **love** sports.
He **likes** practising the piano.	He **likes** music.
I **don't mind** drawing.	I **don't mind** art.
We **don't like** playing chess.	We **don't like** chess.
They **hate** watching TV.	They **hate** TV.

Question forms
Questions with *be*, *have got* and other verbs
Question word + *be* + subject
Why **are you** late? — I'm late because …
How old **is he**? — He's 14.
Question word + *have/has* + subject + *got*
What **have** you **got** in your bag? — I've got my laptop.
How many video games **has** he **got**? — He's got about 50.
Question word + *do/does* + subject + infinitive
How **do** you **go** to school? — I **go** to school by bus.
What time **does** the match **start**? — It **starts** at nine o'clock.

Vocabulary

🔊 17 **Free-time activities**
collect things, draw, go to a dance class, go to the gym, help at home, listen to music, make videos, meet friends, play chess, play football, play in a band, play in a team, play video games, practise the piano, sleep, take photos, use social media, watch TV series

🔊 18 **Collocations with *do*, *go* and *play***
do: aerobics, athletics, gymnastics, hip hop, karate, martial arts, yoga
go: cycling, horse-riding, roller-skating, skateboarding, skiing, surfing, swimming
play: badminton, basketball, hockey, table tennis, volleyball

2 Project

How important are hobbies for teenagers?

TASK: Do a survey about how students in the class spend their free time.

Learning outcomes
1 I can design a survey about free-time activities and summarise results.
2 I can organise a task with my classmates.
3 I can use appropriate language from the unit.

Graphic organiser → Project planner p118

1 Watch a video of students doing a survey. What's the topic of the survey?

STEP 1: THINK

2 Read the survey that the student uses in the Model project.
  1 Find an example of a question which …
     a is a *Yes/No* question
     b gives options for answers
     c is open and has lots of possible answers
  2 Which question word asks about … ?
     a people
     b things
     c time
     d reasons

STEP 2: PLAN

3 Work in groups. Read the tips in the Super skills box and practise saying the Key phrases with your group.

COLLABORATION

Planning and task management

Tips
Agree together how to organise things.
Make clear notes.
Use time effectively.

Key phrases
We can discuss first and then write.
What do you think?
Can you write down our ideas?
Let's write the questions in a different colour.
OK, let's start.
We need to move to the next question.

4 Work in groups of three. Choose a topic for your survey. Use these ideas or your own. Use the tips and Key phrases in the Super skills box.
- creative hobbies (art, painting, drawing, photography)
- music
- social media
- socialising
- sports

5 Write at least six questions for your survey. Remember to include a variety of question types.
Do you like … ?   When do you usually … ?

6 Each person chooses other classmates to ask. Ask the classmates your questions and note their answers.

STEP 3: CREATE

7 Read the summary of results in the Model project. Notice the expressions in bold.

34 Grammar and Vocabulary → Quick review p33

Model project

FREE-TIME activities survey

1. Do you like playing computer games?
   Yes ☐   No ☐

2. What games do you like playing?

3. How many hours a week do you spend playing games?
   1–3 hours ☐   4–10 hours ☐
   more than 10 hours ☐

4. Who do you play games with?
   a brother or sister ☐
   friends ☐
   other people online ☐

5. What is your favourite game?

6. Why do you like it?

FREE-TIME ACTIVITIES SURVEY Class 1B

Most students in the class like playing computer games. **Only four students** say they don't like playing games. **The most popular games are** adventure, action and sports games.

My classmates usually spend four to ten hours a week playing games. **Six people play** 1–3 hours a week, 14 people play 4–10 hours a week and nine people play more than ten hours a week.

They usually play with friends, **but they sometimes** play with people online. **Their favourite game is** the new Spider-Man game. It's fun and exciting.

8. In your group, compare the results of your survey.

9. Read the *How to …* tips on p118. Then write a summary of your results.

STEP 4: PRESENT ●●●●

10. **Peer review** Share your summaries and read other groups' results. How important are free-time activities for students in your class?

2 FINAL REFLECTION

1. **The task**
   Do you ask different types of questions in your survey?
   Is your summary clear and organised?

2. **Super skill**
   Is your group effective at planning and organising work together? Give examples.

3. **Language**
   Do you use language from the unit? Give examples.

3 Dressing up

Why do people dress up?

Vocabulary: clothes and accessories; describing clothes

Grammar: present continuous; present simple and present continuous; time expressions

Reading: a live feed from Comic Con

Listening: a live report about No Uniform Day

Speaking: shopping for clothes

Writing: photo descriptions

Project: make a mini-book about traditional clothes

Video skills p37

Real-world speaking p43

Project pp46–47

Clothes and accessories

1 Read the words in the box. Which ones can you see in the photos?

coat dress hat jacket jeans shirt shoes skirt trainers trousers

2 Read the descriptions. Match descriptions 1–9 to photos A–I.

1. Ajay: a white **T-shirt** with a black and white shirt, jeans and a hat
2. Mickey: a red **hoodie** and black trousers
3. Jenna: a blue and white top with **leggings** and trainers
4. Erin: a white **top**, a pink **scarf**, pink trousers and black **boots**
5. Collection 1: a blue and white top, blue **shorts**, sunglasses, a hat and pink **sandals**
6. Maya: red and black **tights** and black shoes
7. Collection 2: a brown **sweater**, boots, a pink hat, **sunglasses** and socks
8. Nicola: a black jacket, long pink skirt and a hat
9. Louis: a black jacket, a white T-shirt and black jeans

36

Vocabulary 3

5 Complete the sentences with the words in the box.

> boots coat hoodie leggings
> sandals shorts T-shirt trainers

" I love shoes. In summer I wear **1** (…) and when it's cold I wear **2** (…) . And of course, when I do sport I wear **3** (…) . "

" It's very cold today! That jacket's no good – wear your winter **4** (…) . "

" When I go running in summer I usually wear a **5** (…) and **6** (…) , but if it's cold I wear **7** (…) and put on a **8** (…) as well. "

6 💬 Work in pairs. Do you like any of the outfits in the photos?

> I like this one, because I like wearing trainers and it's good for sport.

> I don't like this one, because I'm not into wearing hoodies.

VIDEO SKILLS

7 🎥 Watch the video and answer the questions.
1 How are the clothes you see unusual?
2 Would you like to wear them? Why/Why not?

8 💬 Work in pairs. Discuss the questions.
1 Why is the beginning in black and white?
2 What is the main reason for this video?
   a to be funny   b to sell something
   c to give information
3 What is the message of the video?
   a Fashion is about colour.
   b There are different opinions about what fashion is.
   c Fashion is about art.

3 Match each body part with the words in bold from exercise 2.

Head and neck	
Upper body	
Legs	
Feet	

Plurals

In English, *jeans*, *trousers*, *shorts*, *tights* and *leggings* are plural.
I like these jeans. They're great!

4 🔊 19 Listen to people talking about the photos in exercise 1. Which photo are they describing?

3 Reading and critical thinking

A live feed

1 💬 Work in pairs. Look at the photos on p39 and describe someone's clothes. Can your partner guess who it is?

> This person is wearing a hat and a sweater.

> It's this man here.

> You're right!

2 Look at the photos again and answer the questions.
1 What type of event can you see?
2 What happens there?
3 What type of people go there?

▶ **Subskill: Identifying the text type**
Identify the type of text *before* you read. This can help you predict and understand the content.

3 Look at the text and answer the questions.
1 What type of text is it?
2 Do you normally read this type of text … ?
   a in a book
   b on a computer
   c on your phone
3 What is unusual about the order of the text?

4 🔊 20 Read and listen to the text and match each message with a photo.

5 Are the sentences true or false? Find information in the text to support your answer.
1 Comic Con isn't very busy at the start of the day.
2 The fans walk in slowly.
3 Some people are wearing unusual clothes.
4 In one part of the festival you can watch people draw.
5 Fans can see their heroes but they can't meet them.
6 At Comic Con you can try new video games.

6 **Word work** Match the definitions to the words in bold in the text.
1 people who draw or paint
2 someone who people admire
3 the clothes a person (e.g. an actor) wears to look like a different person
4 the signatures of famous people
5 very big
6 feeling very happy about something

7 The words in bold are in the wrong sentence. Correct the sentences.
1 An elephant is an **excited** animal.
2 Leonardo da Vinci was a famous **hero**.
3 Superman is my favourite comic book **artist**.
4 People wear special **autographs** for Carnival.
5 It's my birthday tomorrow – I'm really **enormous**!
6 Some people like collecting **costumes**.

CRITICAL THINKING

1 **Understand** The reading about Comic Con is a live feed. Choose the correct sentence.
   a We use a live feed to report actions or events when they are happening.
   b We use a live feed to write about general information or things in the past.
2 **Apply** Which of these events could you describe using a live feed?
   • the biography of a famous person
   • a football match
   • your last holiday
   • an election
   • an awards ceremony (Oscars, Grammys)
   • reference information about an animal
3 **Create** Think of two more events you could report with a live feed.

 More than 130,000 people visit the original Comic-Con in San Diego, USA, every year.

COMIC CON

Facts

Comic Con festivals are for people who like comics, video games and films.

Many countries have festivals for comic fans, including the USA, Brazil, the Philippines and India.

Fans often dress up as their favourite characters from science fiction and superhero films.

3:31 pm
Now I'm in the Game Zone. It's the place to be for video games fans. Lots of fans are here and they're having a great time! They're playing this year's new games. More from Comic Con later!

2:47 pm
Comic Con is a great place to see actors, artists and other stars. A lot of fans are getting **autographs** and you can take a photo with your **hero**.

1:54 pm
I'm now in Artists' Alley. People are buying comics and watching their favourite **artists** at work. What's this man doing? He's drawing a comic – it's really interesting to watch him draw.

12:32 pm
A man on the stage has got a hat on and he's wearing striped blue tights. His face is completely white and his hair is orange! Another great costume – he's the Mad Hatter from *Alice in Wonderland*. Fantastic!

12:15 pm
I can see some amazing costumes. One man is wearing an **enormous** green top and brown trousers – wait – he's turning round. He's the Hulk!

12:01 pm
The doors are opening now and hundreds of people are coming through the doors. The organisers are telling people to go slowly but the fans aren't listening. They all want to get in. So many people!

11:25 am
The day's just starting but already a lot of people are waiting to get in. Hundreds of Comic Con fans are arriving and some of them are wearing amazing **costumes**. Everyone's very **excited**.

The longer read → Resource centre

3 Grammar

Present continuous

1 Read the examples. Copy and complete the table with *aren't, isn't, listening, 'm* or *'s*.

> People **are buying** comics.
> He**'s wearing** striped blue tights.
> The fans **aren't listening**.

Affirmative/Negative		
subject	be	verb -*ing*
I	1 (…)	buying … wearing …
You/We/They	're	
He/She/It	2 (…)	
subject	be + not	verb -*ing*
I	'm not	5 (…)
You/We/They	3 (…)	
He/She/It	4 (…)	

2 Read the Spelling rules on p45. Complete the sentences with the present continuous form of the verbs in brackets.
1 They (…) **(take)** photos.
2 I (…) **(play)** a video game.
3 You (…) **(not wear)** a costume.
4 He (…) **(wait)** to get an autograph.
5 She (…) **(not sit)** in the café.

3 Write sentences that are true for you. Use the present continuous.
1 I (…) . *I'm sitting in class. I'm not wearing a hat.*
2 My teacher (…) .
3 My classmates and I (…) .
4 The person next to me (…) .

4 Copy the tables and add the examples in the box.

> **What's** this man **doing**? Drawing a comic.
> **Are** they **having** a good time? Yes, they **are**.
> **Is** he **wearing** a costume? No, he **isn't**.

Wh- questions			
question word	be	subject	verb -*ing*
Where	are	they	going?

Yes/No questions and short answers			
be	subject	verb -*ing*	
Am	I	sitting	in your chair?
Yes/No,	subject	be (+ *not*)	
No,	you	aren't.	

5 Complete the text message conversation between two friends. Write sentences in the present continuous.

> MIA **1** you / do / homework / ? 15.50
> **2** No / I / not. 15.52 LUKE
> MIA **3** What / you / do? 15.54
> **4** I / play / a video game. 15.55 LUKE
> **5** you / watch / the football? 15.56 LUKE
> MIA **6** Yes / I.
>   Liverpool are playing really well! 15.58
> MIA **7** They / win 3–1. 15.59

6 💬 Practise the conversation in exercise 5 with a partner.

7 Answer the question to solve the Brain teaser.

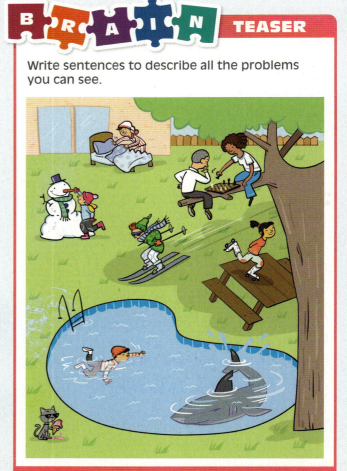

Write sentences to describe all the problems you can see.

What is wrong in this picture?

Pronunciation: /n/ and /ŋ/ → p116

Vocabulary and Listening 3

Describing clothes

1 Match descriptions 1–8 with photos A–H.

1 **tight** jeans
2 a **long** scarf
3 **baggy** trousers
4 **trendy** sunglasses
5 a **thick** jacket
6 **comfortable** trainers
7 **smart** shoes
8 **expensive** boots

2 Match adjectives 1–7 with opposites a–g.

1 smart   a tight
2 thick   b uncomfortable
3 long   c casual
4 baggy   d old-fashioned
5 comfortable   e cheap
6 trendy   f thin
7 expensive   g short

3 💬 Work in pairs. Ask questions about clothes using adjectives.

> Do you prefer casual clothes or smart clothes?

> I prefer casual clothes. Do you like baggy jeans?

A live report

 fun facts Many schools with a uniform have a 'No Uniform Day'. Students pay £1 or $1 to wear their own clothes. Schools use the money for a party or a trip, or they give it to charity.

4 🔊 21 Listen to a reporter for a school radio station. Do the students like No Uniform Day?

1 Ella: yes/no
2 Dylan: yes/no
3 Kate: yes/no

▶ **Subskill: Listening to questions and answers**

In live reports, listen carefully to the questions that the interviewer asks, as well as the answers.

5 Listen again. Copy and complete the table.

	What is he/she wearing today?
Ella	
Dylan	
Kate	

6 Listen again. Complete the sentences with adjectives.

1 Andy thinks Ella's clothes are very (…).
2 Dylan is wearing (…) clothes today.
3 Dylan thinks it's crazy to buy (…) clothes for No Uniform Day.
4 Kate thinks her school uniform is (…) and (…).

7 💬 Work in pairs. What are the advantages and disadvantages of school uniforms? Do you think they're a good idea?

41

3 Grammar

Present simple and present continuous

1 Read the examples in the table and choose the correct option to complete the rules.

Present simple	Present continuous
My friend goes to a different school.	People are arriving.
He doesn't wear a school uniform.	I'm not wearing trendy clothes.
Do you like No Uniform Day?	What's he wearing?

1 We use the **present simple**/**present continuous** to talk about actions that are in progress now.
2 We use the **present simple**/**present continuous** to talk about routines or habits.

Present continuous
We don't use the present continuous with some verbs, e.g. *be, have got, like, love, want*.

2 Choose the correct option.
1 At the moment, I **wear**/**'m wearing** a coat.
2 We **don't go**/**aren't going** to school on Saturdays.
3 It **doesn't rain**/**isn't raining**. We can walk to school today.
4 **Are you wearing**/**Do you wear** the same shoes every day?

Time expressions

3 Find time expressions in exercise 2. Then copy and complete the table with the time expressions in the box.

> ~~at the moment~~ every day   every Monday
> now   ~~on Saturdays~~   right now   sometimes
> this week   today   usually

Present simple	Present continuous
on Saturdays	at the moment

4 Complete the sentences with the present simple or present continuous form of the verbs in brackets.
1 'Can I borrow your dictionary?'
'Sorry, I (…) **(use)** it at the moment.'
2 'What (…) **(Sam / read)** ?'
'It's probably a comic. He (…) **(usually / read)** comics.'
3 '(…) **(your teacher / give)** you a lot of homework?'
'Not usually, but this week we (…) **(study)** for a test.'
4 'Alice (…) **(not sit)** in her usual place.'
'No, she (…) **(talk)** to Kim about their project.'

5 Write questions in the present simple or present continuous.
1 What / you / do / in the evenings ?
2 What / other people in your family / do / now ?
3 What / you / usually / wear / to go out ?
4 What / your teacher / wear / today ?
5 What language / you / speak / at home ?

6 💬 Work in pairs. Ask and answer the questions in exercise 5.

7 Choose the correct option.

GRAMMAR ROUND-UP
1 2 3 4 5 6 7 8

Teenager sells a MILLION dollars … in socks!

It's seven o'clock in the evening. Most kids **1** (…) now, but not high-school student Brennan Agranoff. He **2** (…) new designs for socks.

Brennan **3** (…) about six hours every day on his business. He **4** (…) a computer to make interesting designs and then prints **5** (…) on socks. Then he sells the socks online.

Why **6** (…) he do it? Well, people **7** (…) socks in one colour, and he thinks that's boring. He loves **8** (…) things and he also wants to be an entrepreneur.

Brennan **9** (…) more than 500 designs for socks now, but he plans to create more in the future.

1	a relax	b is relaxing	c are relaxing
2	a create	b is creating	c are creating
3	a spend	b spends	c is spending
4	a uses	b is using	c use
5	a it	b they	c them
6	a is	b does	c do
7	a often wear	b wear often	c often wearing
8	a make	b makes	c making
9	a is	b has got	c have got

Real-world speaking 3

Shopping for clothes

1 Work in pairs. Ask and answer the questions.
1 Do you like shopping for clothes?
2 What are your favourite clothes shops?
3 Who do you usually go shopping with?

2 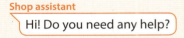 Watch the video. What does Archie buy?

3 Read the Key phrases. Who says them, the shop assistant or the customer?

4 Watch again. Which Key phrases do you hear?

5 Complete the dialogue with the Key phrases. Watch again and check.

Shop assistant: Hi! Do you need any help?
Archie: Oh, I'm **1** (…) a sweater. I like the colour of this one. **2** (…) is it?
Shop assistant: It's £25.
Archie: Can I **3** (…) , please?
Shop assistant: Sure, the changing rooms are over there.
Archie: Thank you! Excuse me, it's a bit small. **4** (…) is it?
Shop assistant: Hold on. It's a small.
Archie: Have you got this **5** (…) ?
Shop assistant: Here you go. It looks good.
Archie: OK, **6** (…) .

6 Create your own dialogue. Follow the steps in the Skills boost.

SKILLS BOOST

THINK
Look at the photos and choose one thing to buy.

PREPARE
Prepare a dialogue. Use the Key phrases.

PRACTISE
Practise your dialogue. Take turns to be the shop assistant.

PERFORM
Act out your dialogue for the class.

7 **Peer review** Listen to your classmates and answer the questions.
1 What clothes do your classmates buy?
2 Do they use the Key phrases correctly?

Key phrases
Do you need any help?
I'm/We're just looking, thanks.
I'm looking for (a sweater/some jeans).
How much is it/are they?
Can I try it/them on, please?
The changing rooms are over there.
It's/They're a bit (small/big/tight/baggy).
What size is it/are they?
Have you got this/these in a (small/medium/large)?
I'll take it/them.

Real-world grammar
I'm looking for a sweater.

Phrasebook → p123

 **3** Writing

Selfie time

Do you like taking selfies? We want to see them!
Write a description of your favourite selfies and tell us why you like them …

A In this photo, I'm standing in front of a blue door. I'm wearing a yellow top, a blue shirt and a hat. I always wear hats! I've got the camera in front of me, so you can't see my face. You can only see my face on the screen. I love taking selfies and I like this photo because it's interesting and funny.

B This is a photo of me with my friends. We don't go to the same school, so we only meet at weekends. We're sitting in front of my house. Jack's wearing jeans and red trainers. Ali's wearing a yellow sweater. Laura's wearing a jacket and green glasses. I'm wearing a T-shirt, trousers and a blue hat. I like this photo because we're having fun.

Photo descriptions

1 Describe the photos. Which photo do you prefer? Why?

2 Read about Selfie time and the selfie descriptions. Why does the writer like each photo?

3 Copy and complete the table.

	Where?	What clothes?
Photo A	1 (…)	*a yellow top,* 2 (…)
Photo B	3 (…)	Jack: 4 (…) Ali: 5 (…) Laura: 6 (…) Me: 7 (…)

▶ **Subskill:** *because* and *so*

We use *because* and *so* to connect ideas in a sentence. We use them when we give a reason or talk about a result.

4 Find two examples of *because* and two examples of *so* in the selfie descriptions. Choose the correct option in the rules.
   1 We use **because/so** to give the reason for something.
   2 We use **because/so** to talk about the result of something.

5 Complete the sentences with *because* or *so*.
   1 It's my birthday (…) we're having a special dinner.
   2 I'm wearing my uniform (…) I'm walking home from school.
   3 I'm not going to school today (…) I'm sick.
   4 It's really cold (…) I'm wearing a coat and hat.
   5 I'm in my room (…) I'm doing my homework.

6 Complete the sentences with your own ideas.
1 We don't have school today because …
2 I don't like sports so …
3 It's hot today so …
4 I hardly ever go to the cinema because …
5 I love photography so …

7 Write descriptions of two of your selfies. Follow the steps in the Skills boost.

SKILLS BOOST

THINK
1 Choose two selfies.
2 Make notes about the photos. Use questions a–f to help you.
  a Where are you?
     in my room
  b Why are you there?
  c What are you wearing?
  d Who are you with?
  e What are they doing/wearing?
  f Why do you like the photo?

PREPARE
Choose which questions to answer and decide the order of the information.
Photo A: *f, c, d …*
Photo B:

WRITE
Write your descriptions.
In this photo, I'm sitting in my room …
I'm wearing …
I like this photo because …

CHECK
Read your descriptions and answer the questions.
1 Do you use the present continuous to describe the photos?
2 Do you use the present simple to talk about habits and routines?
3 Do you use *because* and *so* correctly?

8 **Peer review** Exchange your descriptions with another student. Answer the questions.
1 Does the writer use the present continuous and present simple?
2 Does the writer use *because* and *so*?
3 Which of the descriptions do you prefer? Why?

QUICK REVIEW 3

Grammar

Present continuous
Affirmative and negative
be (+ *not*) + verb *-ing*
I**'m (am) reading** my favourite comic.
He **isn't (is not) taking** photos.

Questions and short answers
(Question word) + *be* + subject + verb *-ing*
What**'s (is)** she **wearing**? A coat.
Are they **having** a good time? Yes, they **are**./No, they **aren't**.
We don't use the contracted form in affirmative short answers.
✓ Yes, they are. Yes, they're.
✓ Yes, I am. Yes, I'm.

Spelling rules
Most verbs: + *-ing* buy → buying
Verbs which end in *-e*: remove *e* + *-ing* take → taking
Some verbs which end in consonant + vowel + consonant: double consonant + *-ing* swim → swimming

Present simple and present continuous
We use the present simple to talk about routines or habits.
We use the present continuous to talk about actions that are in progress now.

Present simple	Present continuous
We usually **wear** a school uniform.	We **are wearing** normal clothes today.
He **doesn't play** football on Wednesdays.	He **isn't playing** football today.
Do you **have** lunch at school? Yes, I **do**./No, I **don't**.	**Are** you **having** lunch? Yes, I **am**./No, I**'m not**.
What **does** he always **do**?	What **is** he **doing** now?

Time expressions
With present simple:
always, sometimes, never, etc., *every day/week/month/year, on Mondays/Tuesdays*, etc., *at weekends*
With present continuous:
now, right now, at the moment, today, this morning/afternoon/evening, this week/month/year

Vocabulary

🔊 22 **Clothes and accessories**
boots, coat, dress, hat, hoodie, jacket, jeans, leggings, sandals, scarf, shirt, shoes, shorts, skirt, sunglasses, sweater, T-shirt, tights, top, trainers, trousers

🔊 23 **Describing clothes**
baggy, casual, cheap, comfortable, expensive, long, old-fashioned, short, smart, thick, thin, tight, trendy, uncomfortable

45

3 Project

Why do people dress up?

TASK: Make a mini-book about traditional clothes.

Learning outcomes

1 I can describe clothes in another country or region.
2 I can use my imagination to present information in an attractive way.
3 I can use appropriate language from the unit.

Graphic organiser → Project planner p119

1 Watch a video of a student making a mini-book. What do you need to make one?

STEP 1: THINK

2 Read the page from a mini-book in the Model project. Which of these things can you see?
- a title
- information about the country or region
- a description of the clothes
- information about when people wear these clothes
- an attractive picture of the costume
- information about the history of the region

STEP 2: PLAN

3 Work in pairs. Choose a region of your country, or another country.

4 Make notes about the following:
- Where is the region or country?
- What are the traditional clothes for men and for women?
- When do people wear these clothes?

5 Find one or more photos or draw a picture of the traditional clothes.

STEP 3: CREATE

6 Work in pairs. Read the tips in the Super skills box and practise saying the Key phrases with a partner.

CREATIVITY

Using your imagination and thinking of original ideas

Tips
Think of different ideas.
Try different options.
Decide what looks best.

Key phrases
What about … ?
What do you think about … ?
We could (write the title in red/put the picture here …)
That's a good idea.
Mmmm, I'm not sure.
That looks/doesn't look good.

7 Read the *How to …* tips on p119. Then make your mini-book. Use the tips and Key phrases in the Super skills box.

Model project

Traditional costumes in BOLIVIA

Different regions of Bolivia have different costumes. Traditional clothes often tell us what region someone comes from.

The Highlands are a region in the west of Bolivia. The traditional costume there has a lot of colours. People wear it for festivals and on special occasions.

Men usually wear a red jacket, a white shirt, white trousers and white shoes. They often wear a hat.

Women have very colourful costumes. They wear long pink, yellow or blue skirts and a hat, and they sometimes wear boots.

In these photos, men are playing instruments and women are dancing in the street during the Laja Festival in La Paz. They are wearing traditional clothes.

STEP 4: PRESENT

8 **Peer review** Exchange your mini-book with another pair. As you read, answer the questions.

1. What new things do you learn about traditional clothes?
2. Does the mini-book have information about the country/region and the clothes?
3. Is the mini-book attractive? Why/Why not?

3 FINAL REFLECTION

1. **The task**
   Does your mini-book describe the region and clothes?
   What details do you include?

2. **Super skill**
   How interesting and attractive is your mini-book? Give examples.

3. **Language**
   Do you use language from the unit? Give examples.

47

4 Extremes

(What do you think?)

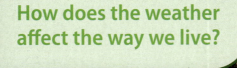
How does the weather affect the way we live?

Nebraska: very strong winds

Seattle, Washington: cloudy for more than 220 days a year

Death Valley, California: sunny and dry, only 6 cm of rain a year

The United States of extreme weather

Vocabulary: seasons and weather; compound nouns: things to take on a trip

Grammar: comparative and superlative adjectives; modal verbs of obligation, permission and prohibition

Reading: a magazine article about extreme places to live

Listening: instructions for an adventure holiday in Yosemite

Speaking: making and responding to suggestions

Writing: instructions

Project: give weather advice to visitors to your country

Video skills p49

Real-world speaking p55

Project: pp58–59

Seasons and weather

1 Write the words in the box in the correct category.

| autumn cold cool ~~hot~~ ~~rain~~ snow ~~spring~~ summer sun warm winter |

Four seasons: *spring*
Four adjectives to describe temperature: *hot*
Three words to talk about the weather: *rain*

2 Work in pairs. Which is your favourite season? Why?

3 Look at the weather map. Match words 1–6 with definitions a–f.

1 ice   a short periods of rain
2 freezing   b with a lot of rain
3 wet   c with little or no rain
4 thunderstorm   d very, very cold
5 showers   e water that is solid because it's cold
6 dry   f violent weather

48

Vocabulary 4

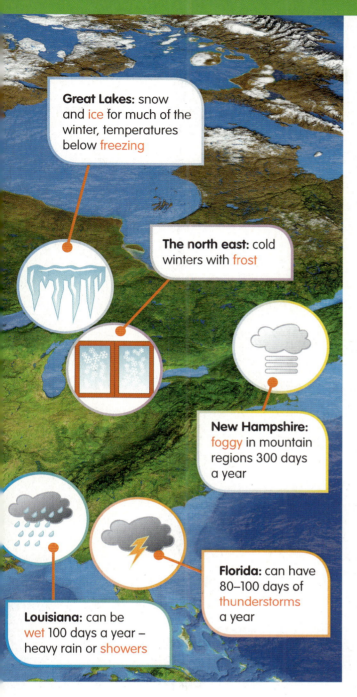

Great Lakes: snow and ice for much of the winter, temperatures below freezing

The north east: cold winters with frost

New Hampshire: foggy in mountain regions 300 days a year

Florida: can have 80–100 days of thunderstorms a year

Louisiana: can be wet 100 days a year – heavy rain or showers

7 Choose the correct option.

In Phoenix, Arizona, it's never cold. In spring and autumn it's warm and **1 sun/sunny**, and in summer it's really hot! It hardly ever **2 rain/rains**, it's usually **3 wet/dry**.

In New York, winters are cold and **4 ice/icy**. Sometimes there is **5 frost/frosty** at night in November and April. In spring, it's often **6 cloud/cloudy**. Summers are hot with the occasional thunderstorm. Autumns are cool and sometimes **7 fog/foggy**.

8  **Work in pairs and answer the questions.**
1 What's the weather like where you live … ?
  a in spring
  b in summer
  c in autumn
  d in winter
2 What's the weather like in the north, south, east, west of your country?
3 What's the weather like today?

9 Watch the video and answer the questions.
1 Why is the video called 'Four seasons in a week'?
2 What things do you need to be ready for the weather in the UK?

10 Work in pairs. Discuss the questions.
1 What do you learn about in the video?
2 What more would you like to know?
3 Why is video a good way to learn about the weather?

4 Copy and complete the table. What letter do we often add to make adjectives?

Noun	Adjective
	icy
sun	
cloud	
	windy
fog	
	frosty

5 How do you say the words in exercise 4 in your language?

6 🔊 24 Listen. What words can you use to describe the weather?

49

4 Reading and critical thinking

A magazine article

1 Look at the photos and read the fact files. What is the weather like in Mawsynram and Oymyakon?

2 Match each word with Mawsynram or Oymyakon. Use a dictionary to help you.

> bridge   freeze   reindeer   roots   umbrella

▶ **Subskill: Understanding the main idea**

The first time you read a text, read it quickly to get a general idea of what it is about.

3 Read the magazine article quickly. What is it about? Choose the correct option.
  a Weather disasters around the world
  b How the world's weather is changing
  c Living in extreme weather conditions

4 🔊 25 Read and listen to the text. Answer the questions.
  1 When does it rain every day in Mawsynram?
  2 What do people put on their heads when it rains?
  3 Why do they make bridges from trees?
  4 What happens to mobile phones in Oymyakon?
  5 What do people eat there? Why?
  6 When do schools close?

5 Are the sentences true for Mawsynram, Oymyakon or both?
  1 People often stay at home in extreme weather.
  2 In some months of the year, it's difficult to sleep.
  3 The days are very short here.
  4 People use plants and trees to help them.
  5 The town is a long way from a big city.
  6 People learn to live with extreme weather.

6 **Word work** Match the definitions to the words in bold in the text.
  1 a loud sound
  2 breaks completely
  3 a type of plant – it grows in a garden or park
  4 a typical amount of something
  5 continue to exist
  6 the top part of a building

7 Complete the sentences with the words in bold in the text.
  1 You can often see birds on the (…) of our house.
  2 My (…) grade at school is 8.5.
  3 What's that (…) ? Are you having a party?
  4 Lessons at my school (…) 45 minutes.
  5 Amy's sitting on the (…) in the garden.
  6 A tropical storm (…) houses and roads.

CRITICAL THINKING

1 **Remember** List the things that are difficult for the people of Mawsynram and Oymyakon.
2 **Analyse** Order the things from most difficult to least difficult in each place.
3 **Evaluate** Decide which is the more difficult place to live in.
Think about:

> clothes   daily routines   food and drink
> free-time activities   houses   transport

Research

Find out what the average temperature and rainfall are where you live.

OUR AMAZING WORLD

Today we're looking at extreme weather in two very different places.

Let's start with Mawsynram in India. It isn't cold there, but it is wet. This is the wettest place in the world. The monsoon season is longer here than in any other place, and it rains every day!

The heaviest rain is at night, so people put **grass** on the walls and **roof** of their homes to stop the **noise**.

They stay at home most of the time in the rainy season. When they go out, they carry bamboo umbrellas over their heads.

They use the roots of living trees to make bridges across rivers. Students use these when they walk to school. The rain **destroys** normal bridges, but these living bridges can **last** for hundreds of years.

Fact file
MAWSYNRAM
Location: north-west India
Population: 237 families
Average rainfall: 11,871 mm

Fact file
OYMYAKON
Location: north-east Russia
Population: 500
Lowest temperature: -71.2°C

In winter, Oymyakon in Siberia is the coldest town in the world. The **average** temperature is -50°C, and it's dark for 21 hours of the day.

Life here isn't easy. People can only stay outside for a minute or two, and they can't make a phone call in the street because mobile phones freeze!

Vegetables don't grow here, so people usually eat meat and drink reindeer milk. They hardly ever go shopping because the nearest city is two days away by car.

In other countries, students don't go to school when it snows, but in Oymyakon, snow and ice are normal. Here, schools only close when the temperature is lower than -52°C!

Life in Mawsynram and Oymyakon is more difficult than in other places, but the people of these two towns find ways to live with extreme weather every day.

The longer read → Resource centre

4 Grammar

Comparative and superlative adjectives

1 Read the examples. Which sentences compare two things? Which compare three or more things?

> Siberia is colder than India.
> This is the coldest town in the world.
> India is wetter than Siberia.
> May and June are the wettest months.

2 Read the sentences again. Complete the rules.

1. To compare two things, use comparative adjective + (…).
2. To compare three or more things, use (…) + superlative adjective.

3 Read the Spelling rules on p57. Copy and complete the table.

Adjective	Comparative adjective	Superlative adjective
cold	colder	1 (…)
wet	2 (…)	wettest
heavy	3 (…)	heaviest
difficult	more difficult	4 (…)
good	better	best
bad	worse	5 (…)

4 Complete the sentences with comparative adjectives.

1. India is (…) **(hot)** than the UK.
2. Wellington in New Zealand is (…) **(windy)** than Chicago.
3. The Antarctic is (…) **(cold)** than the Arctic.
4. Snow is (…) **(good)** than ice for skiing.
5. Thunderstorms are (…) **(dangerous)** than showers.
6. The south of England is (…) **(warm)** than the north.

5 Write sentences about Brazil and Ecuador with comparative adjectives.

1. Brazil / big / Ecuador
2. Quito / high / Brasilia
3. Summers in Brasilia / hot / in Quito
4. Winters in Quito / cool / in Brasilia
5. Quito / wet / Brasilia

6 Complete the quiz questions with superlative adjectives.

WORLD RECORDS

1. Which is *the highest* **(high)** mountain?
   a K2   b Lhotse   c Everest
2. Which is (…) **(small)** country?
   a Andorra   b Vatican city   c Monaco
3. Which is (…) **(hot)** place?
   a Tunisia   b California   c India
4. Which is (…) **(popular)** country for tourists?
   a Spain   b Thailand   c France
5. Which is (…) **(dry)** place?
   a the Atacama desert   b the Sahara desert
   c the Arabian desert
6. Which is (…) **(big)** ocean?
   a the Indian Ocean   b the Atlantic   c the Pacific

7 🔊 26 Choose the correct answers in the quiz. Listen and check.

8 Complete the text with the comparative or superlative form of the adjectives in brackets.

Dubai in the United Arab Emirates has more world records than any other place. The 1 (…) **(tall)** hotel in the world is here, and the 2 (…) **(big)** shopping centre – you can even go skiing inside it! The IMG Worlds of Adventure theme park is 3 (…) **(large)** than any other theme park. It's got some of the 4 (…) **(exciting)** rides in the world too.

People often think that Dubai is 5 (…) **(expensive)** than other cities, but in fact many things are 6 (…) **(cheap)**. It's a great place to visit. Many tourists come here every year and the airport is now 7 (…) **(busy)** than London's Heathrow!

9 Answer the question to solve the Brain teaser.

Antalya and Izmir are two of the hottest places in Turkey. In Antalya, the highest temperature in July is 34°C, on average. In Istanbul, it's five degrees lower. Rize is one of the coolest places in July. The average temperature there is three degrees lower than in Istanbul.

What's the average temperature in Rize in July?

Vocabulary and Listening 4

Compound nouns: things to take on a trip

1 Read the leaflet and answer the questions.
1. What is Outward Bound?
2. What type of activities do they organise?
3. What do people learn through these activities?

> The Outward Bound organisation offers outdoor education programmes for young people and adults in over 30 countries. Courses last from two days to several months and can include canoeing, climbing and camping.
>
> On this one-week expedition, middle school students walk, cook and spend time in beautiful Yosemite National Park. Teamwork and communication are two of the most important things you learn.

Things you need:
- backpack
- sleeping bag
- water bottle
- penknife

2 Write a list of clothes to take on an Outward Bound trip.

3 Read the list of things you need in the leaflet. Can you find them in the photos?

4 Copy and complete the table using words from the box to make compound nouns.

> bag (x2) book (x2) bottle brush (x2) case
> cream knife jacket ~~pack~~ paste ~~towel~~

One word		Two words	
back*pack*	hair(…)	beach *towel*	phrase (…)
guide(…)	pen(…)	sleeping (…)	sun (…)
suit(…)	tooth(…)	wash (…)	water (…)
tooth(…)		waterproof (…)	

5 Match the photos in exercise 3 with the items in the table.

6 💬 Work in pairs. Which other things would you take on a trip to Yosemite?

Instructions

> **Subskill: Using pictures to help you understand**
>
> Before you listen, look at the pictures. Can you name them? What other words could you hear? E.g. *camera*: take photos

7 🔊 27 Listen to a guide at Yosemite Park. Order the pictures.

a (…)	b (…)	c (…)	d (…)	e (…)	f (…)	g (…)

8 Listen again and complete the rules.
1. Please listen to the guides at all (…).
2. You can take (…) but you mustn't take (…).
3. Never give food to any (…).
4. Don't leave any food in your (…).
5. Put your toothpaste in a special (…).
6. It's very sunny and hot so wear a (…) and bring sun cream and a (…).

9 💬 Work in pairs. Would you like to go on a trip like this? Talk about the advantages and disadvantages.

> I'd really like to go. I love the mountains.

> I prefer the city. You haven't got Internet in Yosemite!

4 Grammar

Modal verbs of obligation, permission and prohibition

1 Read the examples. Copy and complete the table with *can*, *can't*, *must* and *mustn't*.

> You can take photos.
> You can't leave any food in your backpack.
> Can we take food into the park?   Yes, you can.
> Can we give food to the animals?   No, you can't.
> All food must go in these special boxes.
> You mustn't take any plants or flowers with you.

Obligation	Permission	Prohibition
1 (…)	2 (…)	3 (…)
		4 (…)

2 Copy and complete the tables with the examples in exercise 1.

Affirmative and negative

subject	can/can't/ must/mustn't	verb	
You	can	take	photos.
1 (…)	(…)	(…)	(…)
2 (…)	(…)	(…)	(…)
You	mustn't	take	any plants.

Questions and short answers

Can	subject	verb	
Can	we	take	food into the park?
3 (…)	(…)	(…)	(…)
Yes/No	subject	can/can't	
Yes,	you	can.	
4 (…)	(…)	(…)	

3 Rewrite the sentences using the words and symbols in brackets.

1. You can take photos. (we / ?)
   Can we take photos?
2. You must bring a small backpack. (you / -)
3. You can phone home at weekends. (I / ?)
4. Can we drink the water here? (you / -)
5. Can we wear shorts today? (we / +)
6. We mustn't eat here. (you / +)
7. You can't wear trainers for this walk. (we / ?)

4 Rewrite the rules using *can*, *can't*, *must* and *mustn't*.

1. It's OK to bring your bike. *You can bring your bike.*
2. It's OK to come in a group of up to eight people.
3. It's very important to come with an adult.
4. It's important that you don't stay in the park overnight.
5. It's OK to visit the park from March to November.
6. It's very important to wear shoes, not open sandals.

5 Read the school rules and rewrite them so they are true for your school.

1. You can use your mobile phone in class.
2. You must run in the school building.
3. You can't use a ball in the playground.
4. You can wear your own clothes.
5. You mustn't arrive before 9:00.
6. You can eat and drink in the classroom.

6 Choose the correct option.

GRAMMAR ROUND-UP
1 2 3 4 5 6 7 8

My family and I **1 go sometimes/sometimes go** on holiday in the Sierra de Guara. It's a beautiful place, but I love **2 it/him** because it's the **3 best/better** place I know to go canyoning.

Canyoning is a fantastic sport to do in spring or summer. First you walk up a mountain with your guide. That's quite difficult because **4 you wearing/ you are wearing** a wetsuit! Then you go down the mountain, but it's **5 harder/more hard** than it sounds because you walk in a river! I think canyoning is **6 interesting/more interesting** than other sports because it's a mix of swimming, jumping from rocks and climbing.

If you're very good, you **7 can go/can to go** alone, but **8 we always go/we go always** with a group. Canyoning is a lot of fun but you **9 must listen/can listen** to the guide because it can be dangerous.

Research
Can you go canyoning near where you live?

Pronunciation: *can* → p116

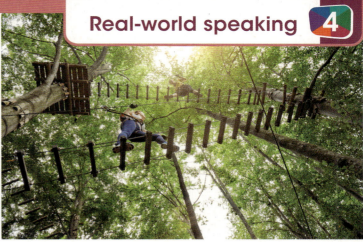

Real-world speaking 4

Making and responding to suggestions

1. Look at the photo and answer the questions.
   1. What can you do there?
   2. Is there a park like this near where you live?

2. 🎥 Watch the video. Is it a school trip or are the friends organising it?

3. Watch again. Which two Key phrases do you not hear?

4. Complete the dialogue with the Key phrases. Watch again and check.

   Kirsty: I'm really excited about our day out tomorrow.
   Sam: Me, too. What time does the zip line open?
   Kirsty: Ummm – 8:00. So I think we **1** (…) get the bus at 8:30.
   Sam: Really? That's too early! How **2** (…) the 9:00 bus?
   Kirsty: OK, **3** (…).
   Sam: Do we need special clothes?
   Kirsty: Ummm – comfortable clothes, sneakers, but you can't wear sandals.
   Sam: What about lunch?
   Kirsty: Why **4** (…) take a picnic? It'll be cheaper that way.
   Sam: Yes, **5** (…). Oh, this looks awesome. It has the longest zip lines in California!
   Kirsty: Look, this one's 2,700 feet long!
   Sam: Amazing!

5. Create your own dialogue. Follow the steps in the Skills boost.

   ### SKILLS BOOST

   THINK
   Think of a place to visit (e.g. a theme park, water park, a stadium…)
   Make notes about times, price, travel, food and clothes/things you need.

   PREPARE
   Prepare a dialogue to discuss options for your trip. Remember to include Key phrases for making and responding to suggestions.

   PRACTISE
   Practise your dialogue.

   PERFORM
   Act out your dialogue for the class.

6. **Peer review** Listen to your classmates and answer the questions.
   1. Where do they choose to visit?
   2. Which Key phrases do they use?

   ### Key phrases
   Making suggestions: We should (go by train).
   Let's (get the bus).
   Why don't we (take a picnic)?
   How about (getting the 9:00 bus)?
   Agreeing with suggestions: OK, fine.
   Good idea.
   Disagreeing with suggestions: Really? That's too early.
   I'm not sure. I don't like (picnics).

   🇺🇸 US ➔ UK
   You can't wear sneakers. (US) ➔ You can't wear trainers. (UK)
   This looks awesome! (US) ➔ This looks brilliant! (UK)

Phrasebook ➔ p123

4 Writing

Get it right: HOW TO PACK FOR A CAMPING TRIP

1 When you go on a camping holiday, <u>it's important to</u> pack your backpack well. It's easier to carry the heavier things at the top. The lighter things go at the bottom of the backpack.

TOP SECTION

2 The top of your backpack is for things you need on the journey. <u>This is a good place for</u> your hat, your water bottle and a snack too. The top section also has space to put your waterproof jacket: it's easy to get it out if it starts to rain.

BOTTOM SECTION

3 The bottom section is the biggest and this is where you pack the things you don't need while you are travelling to the campsite. Your sleeping bag is probably the biggest thing you're carrying, but it's also quite light. <u>It's a good idea to</u> pack this first, right at the bottom. After that, pack your clothes, cooking equipment and the rest of your food too.

Instructions

1 Look at the diagram and read the packing instructions. Order the paragraphs.
   a   The top section
   b   Introduction and general information
   c   The bottom of the backpack

2 Copy and complete the table with the things you pack in each section and why.

	What?	Why?
top		
bottom		

- sleeping bag
- water bottle and waterproof jacket
- clothes and cooking equipment
- because you don't need these things during the day
- because it's big but light
- because you use these things during the journey

▶ **Subskill:** *too* and *also*

To add another idea, use words like *too* and *also*.

3 Find two sentences with *too* and two sentences with *also* in the text. Complete the rules with *too* and *also*.
   1 (…) comes at the end of sentence with a list.
   2 (…) comes after the verb *be* and before other verbs.

4 Rewrite the sentences with *too* and *also* in the correct position.
   1 I normally pack a waterproof jacket and waterproof trousers. **(too)**
   2 I like canyoning and I like going on zip lines. **(also)**
   3 We go to Italy on holiday and to see my grandparents. **(too)**
   4 My suitcase is very big. It's very heavy. **(also)**
   5 I listen to music on my mobile phone and I take photos with it. **(also)**
   6 The sun's very hot today. You must use a hat and sun cream. **(too)**

5 Write instructions for how to pack for a beach holiday. You can take a small bag for the journey (hand luggage) and a suitcase. Follow the steps in the Skills boost.

SKILLS BOOST

THINK
1 Think of things to take on a beach holiday. Divide them into two groups:

Hand luggage	Suitcase
mobile phone	shorts

2 Compare your list with a partner. Is anything missing?
3 Write sentences about packing these things. Use the information in exercise 1 and the underlined phrases from the text.

<u>It's important to</u> put your mobile phone in your hand luggage.

PREPARE
Organise your notes into paragraphs:
Paragraph 1: general introduction
Paragraph 2: suitcase
Paragraph 3: hand luggage

WRITE
Write your instructions. Use the example in exercise 1 to help you.

When you go on a beach holiday it's important to pack your suitcase and hand luggage well.

CHECK
Read your instructions. Answer the questions.
1 Do you use *also* and *too* correctly?
2 Do you use comparatives and superlatives?
3 Do you use modal verbs?

6 **Peer review** Exchange your instructions with another student. Answer the questions.
1 Are the instructions clear and easy to understand? Is anything missing?
2 Does the writer use *too* and *also* correctly?
3 Does the writer use comparatives, superlatives or modal verbs?

QUICK REVIEW 4

Grammar

Comparatives and superlatives
To compare two things, use comparative adjective + *than*.
To compare three things, use *the* + superlative adjective.
Madrid is **warmer than** Santander.
Seville is **the hottest** place in Spain.

Spelling of comparative and superlative adjectives
One syllable adjectives → + *-er, -est*
If the adjective ends in *-e* → + *-r, -st*
cold → colder → the coldest
white → whiter → the whitest
One syllable adjectives ending in vowel + consonant → double the final consonant + *-er, -est*
hot → hotter → the hottest
Adjectives ending in *-y* → *-y* + *-ier, -iest*
sunny → sunnier → the sunniest
Adjectives with two or more syllables → *more, the most* + adjective
beautiful → more beautiful → the most beautiful
Irregular
good → better → the best   bad → worse → the worst

Modal verbs of obligation, permission and prohibition
Use *can* to give/ask about permission.
You **can** ask questions now.
Can we take photos?   Yes, you **can**.
Use *must* to talk about obligation.
You **must** arrive at 9:00.
Use *can't* and *mustn't* to talk about prohibition.
You **can't** use a dictionary.   You **mustn't** eat in class.

Affirmative and negative
Use subject + *can/can't/must/mustn't* + verb.
No change for *he/she/it*:   She ~~cans~~ swim.

Questions and short answers
For questions, use *can* + subject + verb?
For short answers, use *Yes/No,* + subject + *can/can't*.

Vocabulary

🔊 28 Seasons and weather
Seasons: autumn, spring, summer, winter
Temperature: cold, cool, freezing, hot, warm
Weather: cloud, cloudy, dry, fog, foggy, frost, frosty, ice, icy, rain, showers, snow, sun, sunny, thunderstorms, wet, wind, windy

🔊 29 Compound nouns: things to take on a trip
backpack, beach towel, guidebook, hairbrush, penknife, phrase book, sleeping bag, suitcase, sun cream, toothbrush, toothpaste, wash bag, water bottle, waterproof jacket

4 Project

WDYT? (What do you think?)

How does the weather affect the way we live?

TASK: Make a video giving weather advice to visitors to your country.

Learning outcomes
1 I can speak about the weather in my country.
2 I can listen when I work with other students.
3 I can use appropriate language from the unit.

Graphic organiser → Project planner p119

1 Watch a video of a student giving weather advice. Which seasons does she talk about?

STEP 1: THINK

2 Read the notes about Finland in the Model project and answer the questions.
   1 What is the same and what is different from the video?
   2 What information can you see about each season?

STEP 2: PLAN

3 Work in pairs. Read the tips in the Super skills box and practise saying the Key phrases with a partner.

COMMUNICATION

Active listening

Tips
Don't interrupt when your partner is speaking.
Listen to what your partner says.
Repeat what your partner says to check that you understand.

Key phrases
You go first.   OK, let me check I understand.
So you think …   Can you explain about … ?
Sorry, can you say   What do you mean about … ?
that bit again?

4 Work in pairs. Choose a region of your country and make notes about the following (don't write complete sentences). Use the tips and Key phrases in the Super skills box.
   • What is the weather like … ?
     in spring   in summer
     in autumn   in winter
   • What do people do in each season?
   • What is it a good idea to bring at each time of year?

STEP 3: CREATE

5 Read the *How to …* tips on p119. Then decide who says what in your video.

6 Practise saying your part of the video using notes only.

7 Record your video.

Model project

FINLAND
Four different seasons – different but beautiful!

Winter:
December to March, -30°C – 0°C
freezing temperatures, snow
people go skiing, snowboarding, ice-skating
Bring: thick coat, scarf, hat, gloves, waterproof boots

Spring/Autumn:
April to May and September to November, 2°C – 15°C
cool, often windy, sometimes rains
people love walking in countryside
Bring: walking boots, a waterproof jacket, jeans, sweaters, a backpack, a water bottle

Summer:
June to August, 1°C – 32°C
warm and sunny
people spend time outside – swimming, fishing, sitting in sun
Bring: shorts, T-shirts, sandals, sunglasses, sun cream

STEP 4: PRESENT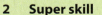

8 <mark>Peer review</mark> Show your video to other students. As you watch, answer the questions.
1. Is the information clear and helpful?
2. When would you like to visit this region? Why?

4 FINAL REFLECTION

1 The task
Can you talk about the weather in your country?
Is the information in your video clear and helpful?

2 Super skill
How well can you listen to other students? How do you know?

3 Language
Do you use language from the unit? Give examples.

Must try!

What makes a town a good place to live in?

Vocabulary: food and drink; places in a town

Grammar: countable and uncountable nouns; *there is/are; Is/Are there ... ? how much/many ... ?*

Reading: a guidebook about local food

Listening: an informal conversation about a visit to Buenos Aires

Speaking: asking for directions

Writing: a description of a place

Project: make a map for young people moving to live in your town

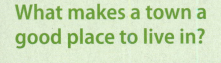

1 (...) : perfection on a plate!

2 I think (...) is really nice

3 Give me some ch- ch- ch- (...)

4 Pass the (...) , please!

Video skills p61

Real-world speaking p67

Project pp70–71

Food and drink

1 ♻ Look at this photo-sharing app for food lovers. Choose the missing food in each text from the words in the box.

| banana   cheese   chicken   chocolate   oil   peas   rice |

2 Copy and complete the table with the words in exercise 1.

Meat/fish	Carbs	Dairy	Fruit	Vegetables	Desserts	Other
🐟	🌾	🍶	🍒🍎	🥕	🧁	🧂

Vocabulary 5

5 Be happy, have a (…) !

6 Keep calm and eat (…)

7 O is for (…)

FUN FOOD FACTS

a (…) comes in more than 100 different shapes; two of the most popular are spaghetti and macaroni.
b Cows are not the only animals to produce (…). You can also get it from sheep, camels and reindeer!
c The United States and Brazil are the world's biggest producers of (…). That explains why burgers are so popular in the USA.
d (…) are similar to pasta. They are popular in China and Japan.
e It takes more than 20 litres of milk to make a kilo of (…).
f A lot of people cry when they cut (…). Some people say it helps to cut them under water.
g (…) is a liquid you put on food. Examples are ketchup and mayonnaise.
h People use (…) like pepper, oregano and curry when cooking to make food taste better.

3 Read the Fun food facts and complete the text with words in the box.

| beef butter cake chips eggs |
| grapes herbs and spices ice cream |
| melon milk mushrooms noodles |
| onions pasta sauce yoghurt |

4 Add the words from exercise 3 to the table in exercise 2.

5 Work in pairs. Can you add any more food items to the table?

6 Work in pairs. Ask and answer the questions.
1 What's your favourite food?

> My favourite food is chocolate. What about you?

> I love bananas! I have one every morning for breakfast.

2 What do you eat for a snack?
3 What food don't you like?
4 What food do you eat on your birthday?

7 Say three ingredients you use when you make …
1 a cake
2 pizza

8 Think of a popular dish in your country. What are the ingredients?

VIDEO SKILLS

9 Watch the video and answer the questions.
1 What cake and drink does she make?
2 What are the ingredients?

10 Work in pairs. Discuss the questions.
1 Why do people make 'how to' videos?
2 Why is this kind of video popular?
3 What could you make a 'how to' video about?

Pronunciation: /iː/ and /ɪ/ → p117

5 Reading and critical thinking

A guidebook

1 🔊 30 Listen to the descriptions. Can you name the food?

2 💬 Work in pairs. Look at the photos on p63. Describe one to your partner. Can he/she identify the photo?

3 Look at the flags. Can you name the country? Do you know any food from these countries?

4 Read the text quickly and name the food in the photos.

▶ **Subskill: Identifying key words**
To find specific information, you don't need to read the text in detail. Look over the text to identify the key words you need.

5 Read the text quickly again. Copy and complete the table.

Dish	Country	Ingredients
poutine	1 (…)	2 (…)
3 (…)	Portugal	4 (…)
5 (…)	6 (…)	chicken, herbs and spices, rice, peas
halo-halo	7 (…)	8 (…)
pad Thai	9 (…)	eggs, noodles, vegetables, beef, chicken

6 🔊 31 Read and listen to the text in detail and correct the sentences.
1 Poutine is a good thing to eat in summer.
2 Pastel de nata is a delicious chocolate cake.
3 Jerk chicken and chips is popular in Jamaica.
4 An ice cream is the best thing on a hot day in the Philippines.
5 Pad Thai always has beef and chicken.

7 **Word work** Match the definitions to the words in bold in the text.
1 very tasty and good to eat
2 a combination of different things
3 something you notice with your nose
4 food you buy to eat in a different place
5 put something extra
6 places (e.g. in a market) where you can buy food to eat in the street

8 Complete the sentences with words from exercise 7.
1 My dad's macaroni cheese is (…) .
2 My favourite (…) is pizza.
3 I hate the (…) of onions.
4 My favourite dish is a (…) of rice, vegetables and chicken.
5 To make ice cream even better, (…) chocolate sauce.
6 One of my favourite (…) sells pancakes with lemon and sugar.

9 💬 Work in pairs. Change the underlined words in exercise 8 so the sentences are true for you. Compare with your partner.

10 💬 Work in pairs. Ask and answer the questions.
1 What can you buy at food stalls in your country?
2 Do you ever buy food to eat in the street?
3 What do you eat if you go out with your friends?

CRITICAL THINKING

1 **Remember** Which of the foods in the text would you like to try?
2 **Analyse** Put them in order from your favourite to least favourite.
3 **Evaluate** What foreign food restaurants are there where you live?
4 Why should people try food from different places? Write a list of reasons.

Research

Choose a country and find out about a typical dish.

HOW TO... EAT LIKE A LOCAL

When you visit other countries, forget fast food like burgers. There is some great local food you must try. Here are some of our favourites!

If you're feeling cold and hungry in winter in Canada, then there is only one thing to eat: poutine. There isn't a better snack! To make poutine, you take some chips, **add** some cheese and cover it all with meat sauce. It's a **delicious** way to get warm on a winter's day.

If you visit Portugal there is a fantastic cake you must eat called pastel de nata. It's a small cake made with eggs and butter. For me there's only one problem with pastel de nata: there isn't any chocolate!

Imagine: you're walking along the road in Kingston, Jamaica. Music is playing and there is a wonderful **smell** of herbs and spices. You're starting to feel really hungry and there's only one thing you want to eat: jerk chicken. There aren't any chips with this **takeaway**. You eat jerk chicken with rice and peas.

The weather is tropical and it's sunny and hot. After a long day you want something cool and sweet. There are two alternatives. The first is an ice cream. That sounds good, but in the Philippines there is something better: halo-halo. Halo-halo is a delicious **mix** of fruit, milk and lots more, but it's also beautiful and includes purple ice cream!

There are some great **food stalls** in Thailand and one of the most popular dishes is pad Thai. The most important ingredients are eggs, noodles and vegetables, but you can add some beef or chicken if you like meat.

5 Grammar

Countable and uncountable nouns

> Some nouns are countable: we can count 1, 2, 3 eggs.
> Some nouns are uncountable: we can't count water.

1 Read the examples. Are the words in blue countable or uncountable nouns?

> It's a small cake.   We've got two bananas.
> I'd like some chips.   I can't see any apples.
> You eat it with rice.   We haven't got any milk.
> Add some beef.

2 Copy and complete the table with the examples in exercise 1.

Singular countable	
Affirmative	**Negative**
a/an + noun 1 (…)	–
Uncountable	
Affirmative	**Negative**
some + noun 2 (…)	any + noun 3 (…)
noun only You eat it with rice.	–
Plural	
Affirmative	**Negative**
some + noun 4 (…)	any + noun 5 (…)
number + noun We've got two bananas.	–

3 🔊 32 Read the interview with Jonah and choose the correct option. Listen and check.

Paula: What do you have for breakfast?
Jonah: For breakfast I have **1 some/an** egg and **2 some/any** chocolate milk. I don't have **3 some/any** fruit in the morning.
Paula: What about lunch? Do you eat at school?
Jonah: Yes, I do. I often have **4 –/a** pasta and **5 some/any** vegetables. After that, I normally have **6 a/an** apple or **7 a/some** grapes.
Paula: And in the evening?
Jonah: I often have vegetables with **8 a/–** rice or **9 a/any** veggie burger. I don't eat **10 a/any** meat or fish because I'm a vegetarian.

4 Write your own answers to the interviewer's questions.

5 💬 Work in pairs. Compare your answers.

there is/are

6 Read the sentences, then copy and complete the table.

	Affirmative	Negative
Singular noun	There is a wonderful smell. There 1 (…) a/an + noun	There isn't a better snack. There 2 (…) a/an + noun
Uncountable noun	There is some fantastic food. There 3 (…) some + noun	There isn't any milk. There 4 (…) any + noun
Plural noun	There are some great food stalls. There 5 (…) some + noun	There aren't any chips. There 6 (…) any + noun

7 Describe what you can see in the lunchbox.
1 There (…) three tomatoes.
2 There (…) a cheese sandwich.
3 There (…) any grapes.
4 There (…) some water.
5 There (…) a yoghurt.
6 There (…) any rice.

8 Complete the text with *there is/isn't* and *there are/aren't*. Use the words in bold to help you.

My favourite lunch is a Bento box.
1 (…) different **menus** so **2** (…) any **problems** finding one you like.
Apart from chicken and fish, **3** (…) a beef **bento box** and if you don't eat meat, **4** (…) a vegetarian **menu** too. **5** (…) **rice** in all the boxes: it's always included.
You can only buy the food to take away: **6** (…) a **restaurant**. And you must get there early. **7** (…) always a long **queue** at lunchtime.

9 Answer the question to solve the Brain teaser.

2nd letter	5th letter	1st letter	1st letter	4th letter
I				

Look at the clues and write the correct letter. Then order the letters to make something you can eat.

What's the secret word?

Vocabulary and Listening 5

Places in a town

1 Match the places in a town with the pictures.

> bike station   bus stop   cycle lane
> department store   fast-food restaurant   juice bar
> library   museum   music venue   skate park
> sports centre   underground station

Cool places to live

What makes a city a great place to live? Schools, public transport, places to eat – these all are important. The city review website has a list of places you can find in the best cities. Which of them have you got where you live?

2 Where do you go … ?
1. to eat and drink
2. to do exercise
3. to enjoy the arts

3 Add one word to complete the places.
1. bus/underground/train/petrol/police/bike (…)
2. town/shopping/sports/medical/city (…)

4 Work in pairs. Take turns to describe a place. Can your partner guess what it is?

> This is a place to do aerobics.

> I know, it's a sports centre. My turn!

An informal conversation

▶ **Subskill: Predicting vocabulary**

Before you listen, think about the words you expect to hear.

5 Read the instructions in exercise 6. What words and phrases do you expect to hear in the conversation?

6 🔊 33   Mia is planning to visit her cousin Ethan in Buenos Aires. Listen and order the things that they talk about.
a   food
b   music
c   sports
d   transport

7 Listen again. Complete the notes.

- sports centre near Ethan – yes or no? **1** (…)
- How many? **2** (…)
- football – yes or no? **3** (…)
- street food near him – yes or no? **4** (…)
- the best way to get to the city centre? **5** (…)
- live music near him? **6** (…)
- things to take? **7** (…) and **8** (…)

I ♥ Buenos Aires

8 Listen again and answer the questions.
1. What other place for sport is there near Ethan?
2. Where can Mia and Ethan go to eat and meet friends?
3. What food does Ethan recommend?
4. What is the fastest way to go to the city centre?
5. Is it dangerous to cycle in the city? Why/Why not?
6. Where can Mia and Ethan hear live music?

9 💬 Work in pairs. What are the advantages and disadvantages of your town or city? Is it a good place to live? Think about:
- places to do sports
- places to eat
- transport
- places to go out

 fun facts   Buenos Aires has 130 km of cycle lanes. That's perfect to explore the city by bike!

65

5 Grammar

Is there … ? Are there … ?

1 Copy and complete the table with *is*, *are*, *isn't* or *aren't*.

Questions and short answers		
Singular nouns	Is there a sports centre?	Yes, there is./ No, there 2 (…) .
Uncountable nouns	1 (…) there any street food?	
Plural nouns	3 (…) there five football teams? Are there any cycle lanes?	Yes, there are./ No, there 4 (…) .

2 Complete the questions with *Is there* or *Are there*.
1. (…) a 3D cinema where you live?
2. (…) any skate parks?
3. (…) any museums?
4. (…) a lot of traffic in the town centre?

3 Write short answers to the questions in exercise 2 so they are true for you.

4 Write the questions for the answers using *a* or *any*. Then write short answers.
1. There's a sports centre near my home.
   Is there a sports centre near your home?
   Yes, there is.
2. There isn't an underground in my town.
3. There are some fast-food restaurants.
4. There aren't any juice bars.
5. There isn't any good live music.

How much/many … ?

5 Read the sentences in the table and choose the correct option to complete the rules.

Questions	Answers
How much traffic is there?	A lot/Some/Not much.
How many cycle lanes are there?	A lot/Some/Not many.

1. We use *How much* with **countable/uncountable** nouns.
2. We use *How many* with **countable/uncountable** nouns.

6 Complete the questions with *How much* or *How many*. Then answer the questions.
1. (…) department stores are there in your town?
2. (…) public transport is there?
3. (…) open space is there?
4. (…) libraries are there?
5. (…) skate parks are there?

7 Write questions with *How much* and *How many*.
1. brothers and sisters / you / got ?
2. homework / you / do / at weekends ?
3. time / you / spend / watching TV ?
4. comics or magazines / you / read ?
5. fruit / you / eat / every day ?

8  Work in pairs. Ask and answer the questions in exercise 7.

9 Choose the correct option.

GRAMMAR ROUND-UP
1 2 3 4 5 **6 7 8**

The happiest city in the world!

Melbourne, Madrid and New York City are all fun places to live, but the **1** (…) place, according to a recent survey, is Chicago. **2** (…) a lot of places to eat, and the city is famous for its delicious street food. It **3** (…) cost a lot. In fact, Chicago is cheaper **4** (…) many other cities in the USA.

There are **5** (…) fun things to do at weekends. You can take a boat on the river or walk around Millennium Park. If you like **6** (…) , you can also see the park by bike. Or why not go to the top of the Willis Tower? You **7** (…) stand outside the building in a glass box. **8** (…) cities offer an experience like that?

1 **a** good	**b** best	**c** better
2 **a** It's	**b** There's	**c** There are
3 **a** don't	**b** isn't	**c** doesn't
4 **a** than	**b** of	**c** that
5 **a** a	**b** some	**c** any
6 **a** cycle	**b** go cycling	**c** cycling
7 **a** mustn't	**b** can	**c** must
8 **a** How much	**b** How	**c** How many

Real-world speaking 5

Asking for directions

1 Look at the map and write the places.
1 It's **opposite** the supermarket.
2 It's **next to** the juice bar.
3 It's **between** the police station and the hotel.
4 It's **on the corner** of West Avenue and Well Street.

2 🎥 Watch the video and answer the questions.
1 Where does Archie want to go?
2 How many people does he speak to?

3 Watch again. Follow Archie's route on the map. Start from 'You are here'.

4 Watch again. Which Key phrases do you hear?

5 Complete the dialogue with the Key phrases. Watch again and check.

Archie: Excuse me. Can you tell me how 1 (…) the library?

Person 1: Let's see. Yes, go 2 (…), along Station Road. Turn left into Well Street. There's a museum on the corner, you can't miss it.

Archie: OK, along Station Road, then left.

Person 1: That's right. Go along Well Street, and 3 (…) the skate park. Then 4 (…) and it's there, near the sports centre.

Archie: Great, thanks.

Archie: Excuse me. 5 (…) a library near here?

Person 2: Yes. Go along this road and turn right. It's 6 (…), opposite the police station.

Archie: Cheers!

6 Create your own dialogue. Follow the steps in the Skills boost.

SKILLS BOOST

THINK
You are outside the school on the map. Choose a place that you want to go to.

PREPARE
Prepare a dialogue.

PRACTISE
Practise your dialogue. Take turns to give directions.

PERFORM
Act out your dialogue for the class.

7 **Peer review** Listen to your classmates and answer the questions.
1 Follow the route on the map. Are the directions clear?
2 How many Key phrases do your classmates use?

Key phrases

Asking for directions: Excuse me. Can you tell me how to get to the (library)?
Is there a (library) near here?
Giving directions: Go straight ahead.
Turn left/right.
Go past the (skate park).
It's on your left/right.

Real-world grammar

There's a museum on the corner.
Is there a library near here?

Phrasebook → p124

67

5 Writing

The Question: What is your favourite place to visit?

My favourite place to visit is Brighton. My cousins live there, and I often stay with them in the holidays.

It's a small town on the south coast of England, but there are lots of things to do. There's a modern part with a department store and busy restaurants, and there's an old part. I prefer the old part because it's full of interesting shops and cafés. My favourite place sells ice cream – it's got more than 20 different flavours.

Brighton's also got a beach. It's quiet in winter, but it can get crowded in summer. I usually go there with my cousins in summer and we play volleyball or swim in the sea. There's a fun fair near the beach too.

I think Brighton is a beautiful and exciting place. I really recommend that you visit it!

Jayden, United Kingdom

A description of a place

1 Work in pairs. What makes a good place to visit? Make a list of things you like.

shops, …

2 Read Jayden's description of Brighton. Would you like to visit this place? Why/Why not?

3 Read the description again and complete the sentences.
1 Jayden often visits Brighton because (…) .
2 He likes the old part because (…) .
3 He likes his favourite shop because (…) .
4 He usually goes to (…) with his cousins in summer.
5 They like (…) there.
6 He thinks that Brighton is (…) .

▶ **Subskill: Adjectives**

Adjectives help to make a description more interesting. Adjectives come before a noun, e.g. *There are a lot of interesting shops.*

4 Find ten adjectives to describe a place in the text.

5 Match the adjectives in exercise 4 with definitions 1–5.
1 new, from the present time
2 with a lot of something
3 with more people than you want
4 without noise or people
5 with a lot of fun activities

6 The words in bold are in the wrong sentence. Correct the sentences.
1 The cafés are always **beautiful** at lunchtime.
2 There are **modern** flowers and trees in the park.
3 Some of the buildings are **small**, but most of them are old.
4 The department store isn't big. In fact, it's **exciting** for a town this size.
5 There aren't many cars or people so it's very **busy**.
6 It's never boring. It's always **quiet**!

7 Write about your favourite place to visit. Follow the steps in the Skills boost.

SKILLS BOOST

THINK
1 Think of your favourite place to visit. It can be a place where you go on holiday or that you visit at weekends.
2 Make notes. Answer these questions.
- Why do you go there?
- Is it big or small?
- What places are there?
- What do you usually do there?
- What can you eat and drink there?
- Why do you like it?

PREPARE
Organise your ideas into paragraphs.
Paragraph 1: The place/Why you go there
Paragraph 2: A general description/Your favourite places
Paragraph 3: Eating and drinking
Paragraph 4: Why you like it

WRITE
Write your description. Remember to use adjectives.
My favourite place to visit is … . I usually go there because …

CHECK
Read your description. Answer the questions.
1 Do you use vocabulary of places in a town?
2 Do you use *there is/are* correctly?
3 Do you use adjectives to describe the place?

8 **Peer review** Exchange your description with other students. Answer the questions.
1 Choose one place you would like to visit. Why would you like to visit this place?
2 Is the description interesting? Why is it interesting?

QUICK REVIEW 5

Grammar

Countable and uncountable nouns
Countable nouns are nouns that we can count.
bananas, chips, eggs, peas
Uncountable nouns are nouns that we can't count.
butter, milk, pasta, sauce

a, an, some/any
With singular countable nouns, use *a* or *an*.
Can I have **a banana**, please?
With uncountable nouns, use *some/any* or no article.
I usually have **some milk** for breakfast. (affirmative)
We haven't got **any butter** in the fridge. (negative)
Is there **any cake**? (question)
We often have **pasta** for dinner. (no article)

there is/are
We use *there is* or *there isn't* before singular nouns and uncountable nouns.
There's a food stall near my home.
There isn't any sauce on the pasta.
We use *there are* or *there aren't* before plural nouns.
There are some great places to buy street food.
There aren't any chips.

Is there … ? Are there … ?
We use *Is there … ?* with singular and uncountable nouns.
Is there a skate park?   Yes, **there is**./No, **there isn't**.
Is there any street food?
We use *Are there … ?* with plural nouns.
Are there any buses?   Yes, **there are**./No, **there aren't**.
We use *How much* to ask about quantity with uncountable nouns.
How much traffic is there?   A lot/Some/Not **much**.
We use *How many* to ask about numbers with countable nouns.
How many museums are there?   A lot/Some/Not **many**.

Vocabulary

🔊 34 Food and drink
banana, beef, butter, cake, cheese, chicken, chips, chocolate, eggs, grapes, herbs, ice cream, melon, milk, mushroom, noodles, oil, onion, pasta, peas, rice, sauce, spices, yoghurt

🔊 35 Places in a town
bike station, bus stop, cycle lane, department store, fast-food restaurant, juice bar, library, museum, music venue, skate park
bus/petrol/police/train/underground station
city/medical/shopping/sports/town centre

Project

What makes a town a good place to live in?

TASK: Make a map showing useful places for young people moving to live in your town.

Learning outcomes
1. I can give information about facilities in my town.
2. I can think about other people.
3. I can use appropriate language from the unit.

Graphic organiser → Project planner p120

1 Watch a video of students presenting a map of their town. Would you like to live there? Why/Why not?

STEP 1: THINK

2 Look at the map in the Model project and add the places to the diagram.

3 Can you add any more places to the different categories?

STEP 2: PLAN

4 Work in groups of three. Decide to create a map of:
  a all of your town
  b a part of your town

5 Work in groups. Read the tips in the Super skills box and practise saying the Key phrases with your group.

CRITICAL THINKING

Considering the needs of other people

Tips
Think about what other people like.
Include ideas for different people.
Think about what young people moving to your town need to know.

Key phrases
Don't forget …
What about somewhere for people who … ?
I think we need something for someone who …
That's a good idea.
There aren't any places for …
Let's add something about (transport).

6 Make your own diagram of places to include (see exercise 2). Use the tips and Key phrases in the Super skills box.

STEP 3: CREATE

7 Make your map. Remember:
- You can copy from an online map if you want.
- Make the map clear and attractive.
- You can include pictures or photos of the places.
- Write information boxes with more information about the places on your map.

Model project

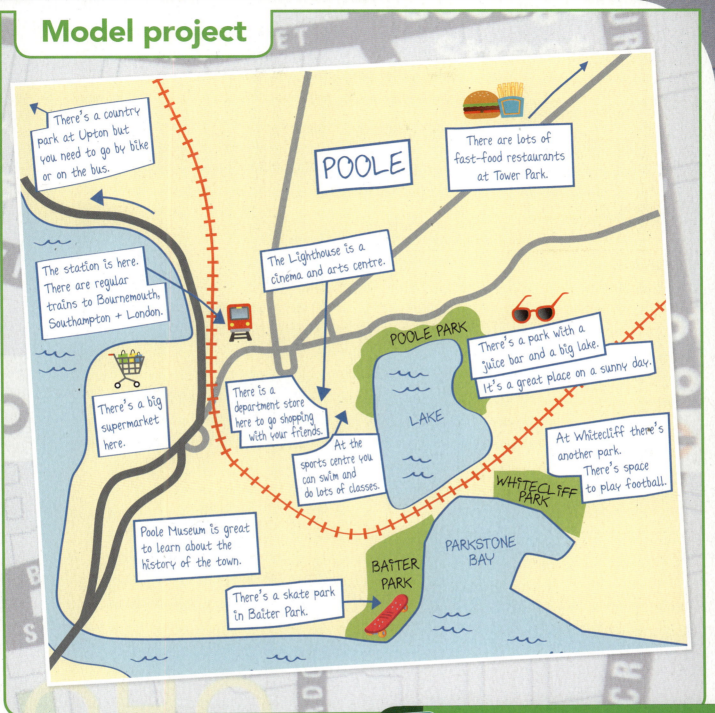

STEP 4: PRESENT ◼◼◼◼

8 Read the *How to …* tips on p120. Then work with another group. Take turns to present your map.

9 **Peer review** As you listen to your classmates, answer the questions.
   1 Do you think the information is useful for young people moving to live in your town?
   2 Ask a question about one of the places.

5 FINAL REFLECTION

1 **The task**
   Is the map clear and attractive?
   Do you give useful information about your town?

2 **Super skill**
   Do you include ideas for different people? Give examples.

3 **Language**
   Do you use language from the unit? Give examples.

6 Animals in danger

WDYT?
(What do you think?)

What can we do to help animals in danger?

Vocabulary: describing animals; collocations: taking action

Grammar: past simple of *be* and regular verbs

Reading: an article about two conservation success stories

Listening: a podcast about a teen entrepreneur

Speaking: showing interest

Writing: an email

Project: prepare a poster about endangered animals

Peacock
Habitat: forest
Description: The peacock has got 200 colourful feathers and a small white beak. It's got wings but can only fly short distances.

Turtle
Habitat: sea, islands
Description: This marine animal has got a hard shell. It can weigh as much as 680 kg.

Goat
Habitat: mountains
Description: The goat lives in mountains. It's got short brown or white fur, a short tail and two horns.

Video skills p73

Real-world speaking p79

Project pp82–83

Describing animals

1 Read the mini texts and add the names of the animals to the table.

Class	Animal	Class	Animal
bird		insect	
mammal	*goat*	reptile	

2 Add the animals in the box to the table. Which animal can't you add? Why not?

> ant   crocodile   parrot   penguin   rhinoceros   shark

3 Read the descriptions and match the words in the box to body parts 1–9 in the photos.

> beak   feathers   fin   fur   horn   shell
> tail   tooth (pl. teeth)   wings

72

Bee

Habitat: garden, the countryside

Description: The bee has got a yellow and black striped body. It makes honey and is very important for plants.

Dolphin

Habitat: sea, rivers

Description: The dolphin lives in the sea. It's got a big fin on its back, but it's not a fish. it isn't up to 100 teeth. It's very intelligent.

Snake

Habitat: deserts, forests

Description: Snakes are often dangerous. This spotted rattlesnake is very poisonous and can kill you.

4 Match the adjectives we can use to describe animals with the correct symbol.

> colourful dangerous marine
> poisonous spotted striped

be and have got

We say 'The tiger *is* a striped animal' but 'It*'s got* (*has got*) striped fur.'

Vocabulary 6

5 🔊 36 Listen to the descriptions and write the name of each animal.

6 Complete the descriptions of animals using words from the box.

> beak colourful dangerous
> feathers horns tail (x2) wings

The parrot is a very **1** (…) bird with yellow **2** (…) on its body. It's got a black **3** (…), blue **4** (…) and a long blue **5** (…).

The rhino has got two **6** (…) and a very short **7** (…). It's a big animal and can be very **8** (…) if it gets angry.

7 💬 Work in pairs. Student A, think of an animal. Student B, ask questions to guess your partner's animal.

Is it a mammal?	No, it isn't.
Is it a bird?	Yes, it is.
Is it colourful?	Yes, it is.
I know – it's a peacock!	Yes!

VIDEO SKILLS

8 🎥 Watch the video. What animals do you see?

9 💬 Work in pairs. Discuss the questions.
1 Why do vloggers make top 5 videos?
2 Why are top 5 videos popular?
3 What could you make a top 5 video about?
4 Do you like this type of video? Why/Why not?

6 Reading and critical thinking

An article

1 💬 Work in pairs. Answer the quiz questions.

How much do you know about extinct animals?

Amazing Animals of the past Quiz

1 Which dinosaur was the biggest?
  a the Titanosaur
  b the Tyrannosaurus Rex
  c the Stegosaurus

2 Was the dodo … ?
  a a reptile b a mammal c a bird

3 Steller's sea cows were very big sea mammals, up to nine metres long! Were they dangerous?
  a Yes, they were.
  b No, they weren't.

4 Were mammoths similar to … ?
  a lions
  b sharks
  c elephants

5 The Tasmanian tiger wasn't a tiger. Was it … ?
  a a dog b an insect c something different

6 Were there any baiji dolphins in Australia?
  a Yes, there were. b No, there weren't.

2 🔊 37 Listen and check your answers.

3 🔊 38 Read and listen to the article about two animals. What do they have in common?

▶ **Subskill: Understanding the content of paragraphs**
Read the headings first, then read paragraph A to see which fits best.

4 Match headings 1–5 with paragraphs A–E in the article.
  1 Can we change this situation?
  2 What are the facts about gorillas?
  3 What solutions were there to the problems?
  4 What is a saiga?
  5 Why were saigas and gorillas in danger?

5 Which animal does the information refer to, the gorilla or the saiga?
  1 In the 1990s, the population was over a million.
  2 They sometimes travel 1,000 km.
  3 There were 500 in 1960.
  4 There were 50,000 in the year 2000.
  5 There were about 200 in the 1970s.

6 Are the sentences true or false? Correct the false sentences.
  1 The saiga has got a very small nose.
  2 The gorilla has got grey fur.
  3 The reasons for changes in saiga and gorilla populations were habitat and hunting.
  4 The populations of both animals are improving now.
  5 The saiga and the gorilla are the only success stories.

7 **Word work** Match the definitions to the words in bold in the text.
  1 a programme of activities
  2 the number of people or animals living somewhere
  3 killing an animal for food or sport
  4 rules made by a government
  5 the place where an animal lives
  6 very hot, dry places

8 Complete the sentences with words from exercise 7.
  1 The Sahara and the Gobi are (…) .
  2 Seas and rivers are the (…) of the dolphin.
  3 I don't like (…) or killing animals.
  4 I'm organising a (…) to get people to cycle to school.
  5 We need more (…) to control the Internet.
  6 The (…) of my city is 700,000.

CRITICAL THINKING   SUPER SKILLS

  1 **Remember** Find examples in the article of actions to help animals in danger.
  2 **Evaluate** Think of an advantage and a disadvantage of each action. Then choose the best idea.
  3 **Create** Imagine you are creating a campaign to help animals in danger. What campaign would you create? Which animals would you help?

The saiga and the mountain gorilla

Two conservation success stories

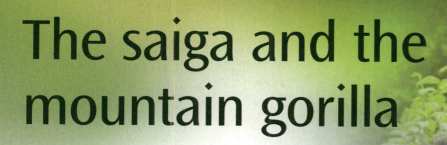

Some scientists say that one species becomes extinct every seven minutes.
What can we do to stop this from happening?
Let's meet two endangered animals and find out.

A (…)
The saiga has got brown or grey fur, horns and a very strange long nose. It lives in groups in the **deserts** of south-east Europe and central Asia. They can travel up to 1,000 km between summer and winter. In the 1990s there were more than a million saigas, but by the year 2000 the population was less than 50,000.

B (…)
The mountain gorilla is a large mammal. It lives in national parks in two regions of Africa. It's got black fur and is very intelligent. In 1960 there were about 500 gorillas in the Virunga mountains, but by the 1970s the **population** was about 200.

C (…)
The saiga and the gorilla were both at risk of extinction. The reduction in **habitat** was a big problem: there wasn't enough open space for the saiga and there was less forest for the gorilla. **Hunting** was also a serious problem. Some people kill gorillas or sell them. There weren't any **laws** to stop this until 2008. Other people kill saigas for their horns.

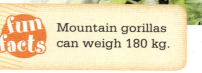
fun facts Mountain gorillas can weigh 180 kg.

Logo of G4G, a mountain gorilla charity organisation

D (…)
Animal conservation organisations, like WWF, and governments were very worried and there was a big **campaign** to help the saiga and the gorilla, with more money to protect their habitats and new laws to stop hunting. There were special exhibitions and there was even a saiga stamp!

E (…)
The saiga and mountain gorilla are still in danger but the populations are slowly growing. And the saiga and the gorilla are not the only success stories: a similar programme is also helping the giant panda. Extinction of plants and animals is still a very serious problem, but with success stories like these, we can see that change is possible.

Saiga postage stamp from Mongolia

The longer read → Resource centre

6 Grammar

Past simple: be

1 Copy and complete the tables with the examples in the box.

> Steller's sea cows **were** very big sea mammals.
> The Tasmanian tiger **wasn't** a tiger.
> There **was** less forest for the gorilla.
> There **were** more than a million saigas.

Affirmative and negative		
Subject	was(n't)	+ singular
Hunting	was	a serious problem.
1 (…)	(…)	(…)
Subject	were(n't)	+ plural
2 (…)	(…)	(…)

there was/were		
There	was(n't)	+ singular
3 (…)	(…)	(…)
There	were(n't)	+ plural
There	weren't	any laws.
4 (…)	(…)	(…)

2 Complete the sentences with the correct past simple form of *be*.
1. The dodo (…) an unusual bird from Mauritius. It (…) one metre tall.
2. Mammoths (…) reptiles; they (…) mammals.
3. By 2002, there (…) any baiji dolphins. They (…) extinct.
4. Steller's sea cow (…) a cow. It (…) a big mammal and its habitat (…) the sea.

3 Read the examples. Choose the correct option to complete the rules.

Yes/No questions	Short answers
Were they dangerous?	No, they weren't.
Was the dodo a bird?	Yes, it was.
Were there any baiji dolphins in Australia?	No, there weren't.
Wh- questions	
What was the problem?	
Why was there a big campaign?	
How many saigas were there in 1990?	

1. In *Yes/No* questions, the verb comes **first/second**.
2. In *Wh-* questions, the verb comes **before/after** the question word (*who, what, why*, etc.).
3. When we ask questions with *there was/were*, the verb comes **before/after** *there*.

4 Order the words to make questions.
1. was / How / big / rhino / the ?
2. dangerous / Was / it ?
3. the / What / rhino's / diet / was ?
4. were / there / rhinos / in / 2011 / many / How ?
5. in Cameroon / there / Were / rhinos ?

5 Match answers a–e to questions 1–5 in exercise 4.
a. Plants.
b. None. They were extinct.
c. It was up to 3.8 m long.
d. Yes, there were.
e. Yes, because it was so big.

6 Complete the text with *was(n't)* or *were(n't)*.

Today on the Fun Facts Forum we answer your questions about

PREHISTORIC ANIMALS

Which **1** (…) the most frightening animal?
Keisha, Boston

I think it **2** (…) the megalodon, from the shark family. Megalodons **3** (…) very dangerous. Their name means 'big tooth'! It **4** (…) a good idea to go near them!

5 (…) dinosaurs the biggest reptiles?
Cameron, Glasgow

Yes, they **6** (…) . But they **7** (…) the most dangerous! There **8** (…) an enormous dinosaur-eating crocodile called Deinosuchus.

9 (…) the dodo the only flightless bird?
Laurie, Vancouver

No, it **10** (…) . There **11** (…) a prehistoric bird that was too big to fly! The Ornimegalonyx was more than 9 kg.

7 Answer the question to solve the Brain teaser.

All the mammoths were in a line. Two mammoths were in front of a mammoth. Two mammoths were behind a mammoth. And there was a mammoth in the middle.

What is the smallest possible number of mammoths?

76

Vocabulary and Listening 6

Collocations: taking action

1 Complete the leaflet with verbs in the box.

> donate   join   organise   protect
> raise   solve   start   visit

Save our wildlife!

There are many ways that we can **1** (…) wildlife. Why not choose two and do them in the next month?

How you can help

- Find out which animals are in danger and what you can do to **2** (…) the problem.
- **3** (…) a wildlife park and see animals in real life.
- **4** (…) an organisation like the World Wildlife Fund and help them with their work.
- **5** (…) a new school club. Meet regularly and talk about animals.
- **6** (…) a special day at your school with games and activities to teach other students about wildlife.
- **7** (…) money to give to a wildlife charity.
- **8** (…) a small amount of money every month and help to save your favourite animal.

2 Match verbs 1–8 with nouns a–h to form collocations.

1	visit	a	a group, a club
2	join	b	endangered animals, birds
3	organise	c	awareness, money
4	protect	d	old clothes, your time
5	start	e	a zoo, a museum
6	donate	f	a party, a sports event
7	raise	g	a mystery, a puzzle
8	solve	h	a new business, a blog

fun facts A typical hive has got 50,000 bees. They make 14 kg of honey. Bees are great navigators. They can navigate like a sat nav.

A podcast

▶ **Subskill: Identifying which statements are true or false**

Before you listen, read the true/false options and underline key words. As you listen, tick the statements that are completely true. The remaining option must be the false one.

3 🔊 39 Listen to a podcast about Mikaila Ulmer. Which two statements are true?
- a She's a young entrepreneur.
- b She donates money to protect bees.
- c She is a volunteer for a wildlife organisation.

4 Listen again. Are the sentences true or false? Correct the false sentences.
1. You can only buy Mikaila's lemonade in Texas.
2. Bees were her favourite insect when she was young.
3. She decided to make lemonade for a business competition.
4. She used a recipe from her aunt's cookbook.
5. Cafés and shops now sell the drink.
6. The President of the USA tried her lemonade.

5 Choose the correct option.
1. Mikaila was **four/five** years old when it all started.
2. She received $ **50,000/60,000** for her business on a TV show.
3. Mikaila has a contract for $ **7/11** million to sell her lemonade.
4. She gives **20/25** % of her money to bee organisations.
5. She visited the White House in **2016/2017**.

6 💬 Discuss the questions in pairs.
1. In what ways is Mikaila extraordinary?
2. What's the most important thing she does?

6 Grammar

Past simple of regular verbs: affirmative and negative

1 Read the examples and complete the rules.

Affirmative	Negative
She started to sell the drink.	She didn't like bees.
She visited the White House.	She didn't stop there.

1 To make the past simple of regular verbs, add (…).
2 To make the negative, use (…) + infinitive.

2 Read the Spelling rules on p81. Write the affirmative past simple of the verbs in the box.

> finish   like   organise   play
> study   travel   visit   watch

3 Complete the sentences with the affirmative or negative of the verbs in brackets.
1 I started my science project last weekend, but I (…) **(finish)** it.
2 We (…) **(watch)** a film about pandas in class yesterday.
3 We (…) **(play)** football last weekend because the weather was so bad.
4 My grandparents are on holiday now so we (…) **(visit)** them last Sunday.
5 I (…) **(like)** animals when I was younger but now I love them.
6 We (…) **(organise)** an event at our school last term to raise money for wildlife.

Time expressions
We use the past simple with past time expressions.
yesterday
last night, last Thursday, last weekend
in August, in 2017

4 Write true sentences for you. Compare your sentences with other students.
1 watch TV / last night
   I watched/didn't watch TV last night.
2 play a computer game / last weekend
3 visit another country / last year
4 study English / last summer
5 listen to music / yesterday
6 travel by bus / last week

Irregular verbs
Some verbs are irregular in the affirmative of the past simple.
go → went   see → saw   have → had   meet → met

5 Choose the correct option.

GRAMMAR ROUND-UP
1 2 3 4 5 6 7 8

Crocodiles of the world

From zoos, to wildlife parks, to city farms, there **1 is/are/were** many places for animal-lovers to visit in the UK.

One of **2 more/the most/the best** exciting places is 'Crocodiles of the World', near Oxford. Here, you can see 150 crocodiles and other reptiles. **3 It was/There was/There were** the idea of Shaun Foggett, or 'The Croc Man'. Shaun had a collection of crocodiles at his home, but there **4 was/wasn't/weren't** space for all of them. He didn't **5 want/wants/wanted** to give the crocodiles to other people so he **6 decide/decides/decided** to start a zoo.

Now, Shaun **7 help/helps/helped** to protect the crocodiles and teach other people about them. Visitors can help to look after the animals – prepare their food and feed them. (You **8 can't/must/mustn't** be careful, of course!) You can also donate money to the organisation.

Research
Where can you go to see animals in your local area?

Pronunciation: Past simple endings /d/ /t/ /ɪd/ → p117

Real-world speaking 6

Showing interest

1 Watch the video and choose the correct option.
1. Megan visited a **city farm/wildlife park/zoo**.
2. Lukas **went out with friends/studied/played computer games**.

2 Watch again. Which Key phrases do you hear?

3 Complete the dialogue with the Key phrases. Watch again and check.

Lukas: Hi, Megan. How was your weekend?
Megan: Hi! It was brilliant! I went to a farm, right here in the city.
Lukas: No 1 (…) ! What was 2 (…) ?
Megan: It was cool! There were loads of animals. Look, I've got some photos.
Lukas: Aww, that's 3 (…) ! 4 (…) funny!
Megan: And this is me feeding the chickens. I wasn't very good at it. They nearly escaped!
Lukas: You're 5 (…) !
Megan: No, it's true! So, what about you?
Lukas: Oh, I was at home the whole time.
Megan: 6 (…) boring!
Lukas: I know, but I finished my science project.
Megan: Oh, no! Is that for today?

4 🔊 40 Listen and repeat the Key phrases. Pay attention to the intonation.

5 Create your own dialogue. Follow the steps in the Skills boost.

SKILLS BOOST

THINK
Choose a place in the town or the countryside that you visited. Make notes about it.

PREPARE
Prepare a dialogue. Include Key phrases for showing interest.

PRACTISE
Practise your dialogue. Remember to use intonation to show interest.

PERFORM
Act out your dialogue for the class.

6 **Peer review** Listen to your classmates and answer the questions.
1. Which Key phrases do they use?
2. Do they use intonation to show interest?

Key phrases

Asking questions: What was it like?
Was it fun?
Responding: You're (kidding/joking)!
Really? No way!
That's so funny!
That's (amazing/cute/great)!
Sounds (boring/interesting/incredible)!

Real-world grammar

There **were** loads of animals.
It **was** cool!

Phrasebook → p124

6 Writing

Josef To: Sam Friday Attachments 1.4MB

Hi Sam,

How are things? We went on a school trip to the National Aquarium last week. It was brilliant! There were loads of fish. The sharks were definitely the best!

First of all, we visited the local fish section and learned about their habitats. Then we saw the jellyfish. They were really cool, especially the white-spotted jellyfish. After that, we went to the Atlantic Ocean tank. It's the biggest tank in the country and we actually walked under the water. There were sharks and stingrays above our heads. It was amazing!

Next, there were the smaller tanks with colourful tropical fish and a giant octopus. Finally, we saw the turtles before we went home. I'm sending you a picture of one of them. I hope you like it!

Anyway, that's all for now. Let me know your news.

Speak soon,

Josef

An email

1 Read the email about a school trip to an aquarium and answer the questions.
1. What marine animals does Josef mention?
2. What adjectives does he use to give his opinion?

2 Read the email again and answer the questions.
1. When was Josef's trip?
2. What was his favourite marine animal?
3. What fish were there in the first section?
4. Which jellyfish was especially cool?
5. What two things were special about the Atlantic Ocean tank?
6. Were there tropical fish in the last tank?

3 Order the places that Josef visited.
a the jellyfish
b the turtles
c the section with local fish
d the smaller tanks
e the Atlantic Ocean tank

▶ **Subskill: Sequencing words**

We use sequencing words to describe the order of events, e.g. *First of all, …*

4 Find five sequencing words or phrases in Josef's email.

5 Read the plan for a visit to a theme park. Write sentences using sequencing words and the past simple.

Last week, we went on a trip to a theme park. It was brilliant! First …

Theme park visit

10.30	Visit the 'Lost Kingdom' section and see 'living' dinosaurs
11.00	Go on the two giant rollercoasters there
13.00	Have lunch in the picnic area
13.45	Walk to the water attractions and go on the water slides
15.30	Meet in the animal arena and watch the keepers feed the penguins

6 Write an email about a trip. Follow the steps in the Skills boost.

SKILLS BOOST

THINK
1 Choose a place that you visited.
2 Make notes about where you went and the things you saw.

PREPARE
Organise your notes into paragraphs:
Paragraph 1: Where?
When?
Your favourite thing
Paragraphs 2 and 3: The places you went to and the things you saw

WRITE
Write your email. Use the example in exercise 1 to help you.
Hi …
How are things? I/We went on a trip to …

CHECK
Read your email. Answer the questions.
1 Do you use *was/were* correctly?
2 Do you use the past simple ending of regular verbs?
3 Do you use irregular verbs in the past?
4 Do you use sequencing words, e.g. *First of all, …, Then … ?*

7 **Peer review** Exchange your email with another student. Answer the questions.
1 Does the writer use the past simple and sequencing words?
2 Would you like to visit this place? Why/Why not?

QUICK REVIEW 6

Grammar

Past simple: *be*
I/He/She/It was/wasn't …
*The Titanosaur **was** the biggest dinosaur.*
You/We/They were/weren't …
*Mammoths **weren't** elephants.*
(Question word) + was/were + subject
Were mammoths big?   Yes, they **were**./No, they **weren't**.
How big **were** they?

there was/were
There was/wasn't + singular/uncountable noun
There was a problem.
There were/weren't + plural noun
There were only 50,000 saigas.
Was there + singular noun ?   Yes, there was.
                              No, there wasn't.
Was there a big population?   No, **there wasn't**.
Were there + plural noun ?   Yes, there were.
                             No, there weren't.
Were there saigas in Europe?   Yes, **there were**.

Past simple: regular verbs
Affirmative: verb + -ed
*She start**ed** a business.*
Negative: didn't (did not) + infinitive
*They **didn't visit** a wildlife park.*

Spelling rules
For most regular verbs, add -ed   visit → visit**ed**
Verbs ending in -e → + -d   receive → receiv**ed**
Verbs ending in a consonant + -y → y̶ + -ied
carry → carr**ied**
Some verbs ending in consonant + vowel + consonant → double the final consonant + -ed
stop → stop**ped**   travel → travel**led**

Vocabulary

🔊 41 **Animals**
Birds: parrot, peacock, penguin   Fish: shark
Mammals: dolphin, goat, rhinoceros   Insects: ant, bee
Reptiles: crocodile, snake, turtle

🔊 42 **Describing animals**
Body parts: beak, feathers, fin, fur, horn, shell, tail, tooth (pl. teeth), wings
Adjectives: colourful, dangerous, marine, poisonous, spotted, striped

🔊 43 **Collocations: taking action**
donate money/old clothes/your time
join a club/a group/an organisation
organise a party/special day/sports event
protect birds/endangered animals/wildlife
raise awareness/money
solve a mystery/problem/puzzle
start a blog/business/school club
visit a museum/wildlife park/zoo

6 Project

WDYT? (What do you think?)

What can we do to help animals in danger?

TASK: Prepare a poster about endangered animals to raise awareness and help to protect them.

Learning outcomes
1 I can present clear information about endangered animals.
2 I can listen to my classmates' opinions.
3 I can use appropriate language from the unit.

Graphic organiser → Project planner p120

1 Watch a video of a student presenting a poster about endangered animals. Which animal(s) is it about?

STEP 1: THINK ◼◻◻◻

2 Read the student's poster in the Model project. Which information does it include?
- a description of the animal
- its habitat
- its population (past and present)
- why it is in danger
- how the animal helps humans
- ways to help

3 Which of these things does the poster in the Model project include to make it interesting and attractive?
- title(s)
- pictures or photos
- maps
- diagrams
- text in short paragraphs
- numbers and statistics
- different fonts and colours

STEP 2: PLAN ◼◼◻◻

4 Work in pairs and choose a class of animal to research.

5 Work individually. Research two endangered animals and make notes. Include the information in exercise 2.

STEP 3: CREATE ◼◼◼◻

6 Work in pairs. Read the tips in the Super skills box and practise saying the Key phrases with a partner.

COLLABORATION

Listening to other people's opinions

Tips
Listen to others and ask questions.
Make decisions together.

Key phrases
That's a good idea.
Yes, that sounds good!
What do you think, (Miguel)?
Why do you think (this animal) is important?
Why don't we choose (the dolphin)?
Do we all agree?
So we've decided that …

7 Work in your pair. Share your research and choose two animals to present. Use the tips and Key phrases in the Super skills box.

8 Create your poster and prepare to talk about it.

Model project

Red pandas

Red pandas live in the forests of China, India, Nepal and Myanmar. They've got red fur with black legs and a white striped face.

Red pandas are in danger because their natural habitat is disappearing, and with it, bamboo, their main food.

Fifty years ago, there were about 20,000 red pandas in the world, but now there are less than 10,000 (and some scientists say only 2,500).

To help to save them, you can join a wildlife organisation and adopt a red panda, or campaign to stop the destruction of forests in Asia.

Sea otters

Sea otters are the smallest marine mammal, but they've got very strong tails to help them swim. They live in the seas around Japan, Alaska, California and Mexico.

In the 1700s, there were between 150,000 and 300,000 of these otters, but people hunted them for their fur. In 1911, they were almost extinct.

The number of otters is growing again (there are about 100,000), but plastic in the oceans is now a problem. We need to teach people about plastic, and help to clean our beaches.

STEP 4: PRESENT

9 Read the *How to …* tips on p120. Then present your poster to the class.

10 **Peer review** Listen to the presentations of your classmates and answer the questions.
   1 Which animal do you like best? Why?
   2 Think of a question to ask about the animals.

6 FINAL REFLECTION

1 **The task**
   How attractive is your poster?
   How easy is it to understand the presentation?
2 **Super skill**
   How well do you collaborate? Give examples.
3 **Language**
   Do you use language from the unit? Give examples.

83

7 Heroes

What makes a hero?

Vocabulary: jobs; adjectives to describe people

Grammar: past simple of irregular verbs; question forms and *ago*

Reading: a newspaper article about teen heroes

Listening: a podcast about two talented teens

Speaking: giving opinions

Writing: a biography

Project: make a presentation about a hero from the past

Video skills p85

Real-world speaking p91

Project pp94–95

CAPTAIN MARVEL

Name: Carol Danvers
Day job: 2 (...)
Job description: She flies an aeroplane.

BATMAN

Name: Bruce Wayne
Day job: 1 (...)
Job description: He's very rich and has got his own company.

SUPERMAN

Name: Clark Kent
Day job: 3 (...)
Job description: He writes newspaper articles for the Daily Planet.

Jobs

1 Who am I? Match sentences 1–7 with the jobs in the box. There are three extra jobs.

> actor   artist   dentist   doctor   police officer
> receptionist   singer   taxi driver   teacher   waiter

1 I work in a school. I give lessons to students.
2 I drive a car. I take people to different places.
3 I paint and draw and make pictures.
4 I work in a restaurant. I bring food to customers.
5 I look after people's teeth.
6 I protect people and investigate crimes.
7 I greet people when they arrive at a hotel or office.

2 Write sentences for the three extra jobs.

3 ◀)) 44 Complete the day jobs of the six superheroes. Listen and check.

> businessman   engineer   journalist   photographer   pilot   scientist

Vocabulary 7

SHURI

Name: Shuri
Day job: 4 (...)
Job description: She invents things in her laboratory.

SPIDER-MAN

Name: Peter Parker
Day job: 5 (...)
Job description: He takes photos for a newspaper.

IRON MAN

Name: Tony Stark
Day job: 6 (...)
Job description: He designs new technology.

Job suffixes
Jobs often end in -er, -or, -ist and -ant.
manager, *teach**er***
*act**or***
*art**ist***
*account**ant***

6 Find other jobs ending in *-er*, *-or*, *-ist* and *-ant*.

7 💬 Work in pairs. Ask *yes/no* questions to guess the job.

> Do you work in an office?
>> No, I don't.
> Do you work in a restaurant?
>> Yes, I do.
> Do you cook food?
>> No, I don't.
> Are you a waiter?
>> Yes, I am!

VIDEO SKILLS

8 🎥 Watch the video. What's the woman's job?

9 💬 Work in pairs. Discuss the questions.
1 What kind of video is this?
   a a mini-documentary   b a vlog
   c an advert for a car
2 Which adjectives would you use to describe the video: interesting, boring, exciting, funny?
3 Who do you think would like this video?
4 How does the video make the woman interesting? Think about: how long you see each image, the sound effects, the voiceover, etc.

4 Match 1–8 with a–h to make sentences.

1	A sales assistant	a	repairs cars and machines.
2	A chef	b	looks after sick people.
3	A web designer	c	sells things in a shop.
4	A manager	d	organises other workers.
5	A mechanic	e	cooks in a restaurant.
6	An accountant	f	works with money.
7	A nurse	g	makes websites.
8	A lawyer	h	helps people with legal problems.

5 Write jobs for each category.
1 **Five** people who wear a uniform or special clothes.
   police officer, ...
2 **Four** people who work in an office.
3 **Three** people who help people with their health.
4 **Two** people who work in a restaurant.
5 **One** person who works with machines.

Pronunciation: Schwa /ə/ → p117

7 Reading and critical thinking

A newspaper article

1 💬 **Work in pairs. Answer the questions.**
1. What jobs help other people? (doctor, police officer …)
2. Which three jobs do you think help people most? Why?

2 Look at the photos on p87 and answer the questions.
1. What was the weather like?
2. What problems do you think people had?
3. What jobs are important in these situations?

3 Read the article quickly and choose the best headline.

A. **Police officers help people after storm**

B. **TEEN HEROES RESCUE NEIGHBOURS**

C. **The people of Texas – the real heroes!**

4 🔊 45 **Read and listen to the article and answer the questions.**
1. Where was the storm?
2. What problems did people have after the storm?
3. Who were the teenage heroes?
4. How did they rescue people?
5. How many people did they rescue?
6. Did they only rescue people?

5 Read the text again. Complete the sentences.
1. When Thomas woke up, he saw that houses (…).
2. He used his boat because (…).
3. Thomas and his friends went to houses when they heard (…).
4. At first, the boys rescued people (…).
5. After several hours, they also worked with (…).
6. People called the boys heroes after a photographer (…).

▶ **Subskill: Understanding new words**
You can sometimes guess the meaning of new words in a text. Think about the general meaning of the sentence. Look at the words that come before and after the new word. Think about what type of word it is (adjective, verb, noun).

6 **Word work** **Find the words in bold in the text. What type of words are they? Can you guess their meaning?**

7 Match the definitions to the words in bold in the text.
1. an adjective to describe a place or situation that is not dangerous
2. people who live in a town or city
3. an adjective to describe a person who does something in a dangerous situation
4. organisations that help people in dangerous situations
5. people who live near you
6. energy that makes light or machines work

8 Complete the sentences with words from exercise 6.
1. We can't use the computers today because there's no (…).
2. I'm not afraid to go out at night. I live in a (…) place.
3. You must be (…) to go to a new country alone.
4. We saw one of our (…) in the crowd of people at the concert.
5. The (…) of Texas are called Texans.
6. There are (…) to help people who get lost in the mountains.

CRITICAL THINKING

1. **Understand** In what ways were the boys heroes? Find examples in the text.
2. **Apply** Do you think we can all be heroes in our daily lives? How can we do this? Think about:
   - at school
   - in free-time activities
   - during the holidays
3. **Evaluate** What other examples of ordinary heroes can you think of? Why do you think they are heroes?

SUPER SKILLS

THE DAILY WIRE

Houston, Texas • 25th April

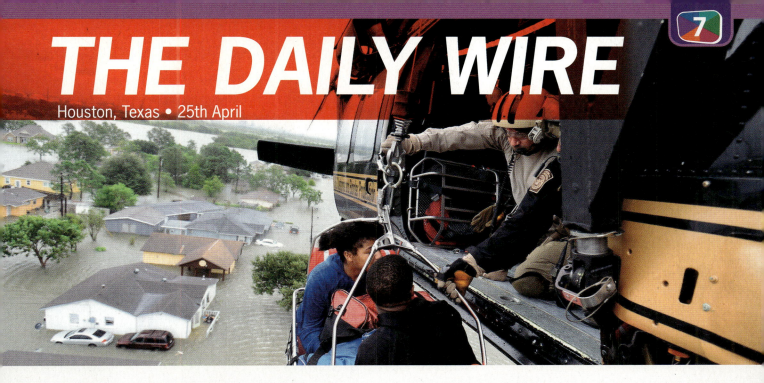

When Storm Harvey came to Texas, it destroyed houses and roads. About 30,000 people left their homes before the storm, but others stayed. They didn't have drinking water or **electricity**, and they couldn't go outside because the streets were like rivers! In those difficult times, the **brave** Texan people helped each other, and many ordinary **citizens** became local heroes.

Among them were four teenage boys: 17-year-old Thomas Edwards and his friends, Richard, 17, Liam, 17 and his brother Declan, 15.

The boys spent hours rescuing their neighbours.

The houses and streets of Texas under water after Storm Harvey

Thomas told journalists that he woke up that morning and saw houses under water. His car was under water too, but luckily, he had a small fishing boat. He rang his friends and they decided to go out in the boat.

They began to look for people and take them to a **safe** place. Sometimes they heard calls for help. Other times, **neighbours** gave them addresses, or directions to the homes of family and friends.

For several hours, the boys worked alone, going from house to house. Later, they helped police officers and **rescue services**. In total, they saved at least 50 people, and even more pets. 'We rescued families, babies, dogs, rabbits,' said Thomas.

A photographer for a local newspaper saw the boys, and he posted photos of them on social media. People wrote comments, calling them heroes. Later, the boys said they didn't do it because they wanted to be heroes. They just wanted to help.

For us, they are true local heroes!

7 Grammar

Past simple of irregular verbs: affirmative and negative

1 Read the examples. Which of the verbs in blue are irregular?

> Thomas woke up that morning and saw houses under water.
> He had a small boat.
> They decided to go out in the boat.

2 Copy and complete the table with the affirmative or negative past simple form of the verbs in blue.

Affirmative	Negative
People left their homes.	Others didn't leave.
Thomas **1** (…) early.	He didn't wake up late.
He had a small boat.	They **2** (…) electricity.
He **3** (…) houses under water.	He didn't see the streets.

3 Write the affirmative past simple form of the irregular verbs in the box. Check your answers on pp126–127.

> begin   come   give   ring
> see   spend   take   wake up

4 Complete the sentences with some of the verbs in exercise 3.
1 There was a storm and I (…) to feel afraid.
2 We (…) people on the roofs of houses.
3 I (…) a friend on my mobile.
4 He (…) to our house and (…) us to a safe place.

5 Rewrite the underlined information in the text. Change the verbs from affirmative to negative and negative to affirmative.

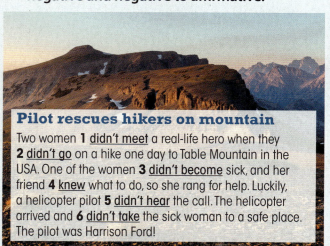

Pilot rescues hikers on mountain
Two women **1** didn't meet a real-life hero when they **2** didn't go on a hike one day to Table Mountain in the USA. One of the women **3** didn't become sick, and her friend **4** knew what to do, so she rang for help. Luckily, a helicopter pilot **5** didn't hear the call. The helicopter arrived and **6** didn't take the sick woman to a safe place. The pilot was Harrison Ford!

6 Write sentences in the affirmative or negative past simple so they are true for you.
1 I / meet / friends last Saturday
I didn't meet friends last Saturday. I went to a museum with my brother.
2 I / see / a film on TV last weekend
3 I / wake up / before nine o'clock on Sunday
4 We / have / pizza for dinner last week
5 I / spend / two hours doing homework last night

7 💬 Work in pairs. Compare your sentences in exercise 6. How many are the same?

8 Complete the article with regular and irregular verbs.

Celebrity heroes

For me, Emma Watson is a hero in films and in real life. After the Harry Potter films **1** (…) **(come)** to an end, she **2** (…) **(be)** a millionaire. She **3** (…) **(decide)** she **4** (…) **(not want)** to just stay at home, so she **5** (…) **(go)** to university and **6** (…) **(study)** literature. Then she **7** (…) **(spend)** time in Zambia and Bangladesh promoting education for girls. She **8** (…) **(become)** a Goodwill Ambassador for the United Nations. She also **9** (…) **(give)** a million dollars to charity.
Emma Watson's career **10** (…) **(not stop)** after Harry Potter. Now she also works to solve world problems.

9 Answer the question to solve the Brain teaser.

A father and two children wanted to cross a river in a boat. The father weighed 90 kilos and each child weighed 45 kilos. The boat could only carry 90 kilos.
How did they cross the river?

Vocabulary and Listening 7

Adjectives to describe people

1 Read the dictionary definitions. Choose the correct adjective to describe people A–C.

generous *(adj.)* giving people more of your time or money than is usual
lazy *(adj.)* not wanting to work
talented *(adj.)* very good at something

2 Match the adjectives in the box with the definitions. Are the adjectives positive or negative?

careful   friendly   kind   polite   special

1 You aren't rude; you say 'please' and 'thank you'.
2 You're different, usually better, than what is normal.
3 You think about what you are doing and try to avoid problems.
4 You like to be with other people and make them feel happy.
5 You think about other people and you always try to help them.

3 Match the words in the box with the adjectives in exercise 2 to make opposites.

careless   normal   rude   unfriendly   unkind

4 Choose an adjective to describe each person.
1 Helen's good at all kinds of sports, especially tennis.
2 My granddad never drives fast and he respects other drivers.
3 Lara gives her money and her time to help others.
4 Ben never plays with his younger sister and he gets very impatient with her.
5 My brother never helps with the housework.
6 Alex often makes spelling mistakes because he doesn't check his homework.

A podcast

5 💬 Work in pairs. Look at the photos and describe what you can see.

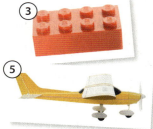 

6 🔊 46 Listen to the podcast. Complete each sentence with the name Easton or Amineh.
1 (…) is from Colorado.
2 (…) is from Syria.
3 (…) moved to a different country.
4 (…) tried to help someone.
5 (…) started a business.
6 (…) won a competition.

▶ **Subskill: Listening for numbers**
Say the numbers in your head before you listen. You'll notice them better when listening.

7 Listen again. Match each number with the correct information. There are two explanations you do not need.

| 14   16   7 $80,000 $600 |
13   £1,000   1 year ago

1 normal cost of a robot hand
2 Easton's age when he met Momo
3 Amineh's age
4 number of robot hands Easton makes in a year
5 when Amineh started speaking English
6 number of people in Amineh's family
7 cost of Easton's hand
8 age when Easton made his first robot hand
9 prize in the poetry competition
10 Momo's age

8 💬 Discuss in pairs.
1 Which person is more impressive?
2 Can we describe Easton and Amineh as heroes? Why/Why not?

89

7 Grammar

Past simple: question forms and *ago*

1 Copy and complete the tables with the words in the box.

| question word   verb   *Did*   *Yes/No*   *did* |

Yes/No questions and short answers		
1 (…)	subject	2 (…) ?
Did	it	cost a lot?
Did	she	speak English?
3 (…)	subject	did/didn't
Yes,	it	did.
No,	she	didn't.

Wh- questions			
4 (…)	5 (…)	subject	verb
When	did	they	move?

2 Order the words to make questions.
1. Easton / What / design / did ?
2. Amineh / a poem / Did / write ?
3. feel / How / Easton / did ?
4. cost / Momo's hand / did / How much ?
5. Amineh / speak / Did / in Syria / English ?

3 Rewrite the sentences as questions with the words in brackets.
1. I got up at 7:30 am. (What time …)
2. I watched TV at breakfast. (Did …)
3. I went to school by bus. (How …)
4. I had spaghetti for lunch. (What …)
5. I saw my friends after school. (Who …)

4 Work in pairs. Ask your partner about what they did yesterday using the questions in exercise 3.

5 Order the time words in the box from shortest to longest.

| day   hour   minute   month   second   week   year |

ago
We use *ago* to say when we did something in the past. We can use different time words:
When did you start this class?
Ten minutes ago. An hour ago.

6 Work in pairs. Combine words or phrases from each circle to make questions. Then ask your partner.

1 When did you

2 start   have   wake up   go

3 at this school   this class   breakfast   on your last holiday   dinner last night   today

7 Choose the correct option.

GRAMMAR ROUND-UP
1 2 3 4 5 6 7 **8**

Yash Gupta 1 (…) in Los Angeles. He started wearing glasses when he 2 (…) five years old and he 3 (…) see well without them. When he was in high school, Yash broke his glasses in his taekwondo class and he didn't have 4 (…) glasses for a week. Yash realised how important his glasses were. He started thinking about people in other countries and he 5 (…) online that more than 12 million children do not have the glasses they need. When Yash 6 (…) 14, he started an organisation called Sight Learning. The organisation collects old glasses and sends 7 (…) to children in 8 (…) countries. Today more than 48,000 children can see better thanks to Sight Learning's glasses.

	a	b	c
1	living	live	lives
2	was	were	is
3	can't to	can't	doesn't can
4	some	any	many
5	reads	read	reading
6	was	ago	were
7	it	them	they
8	more poor	poorest	poorer

Research
Is there somewhere people can donate glasses where you live?

Real-world speaking 7

Giving opinions

1 Look at the photos and think of words you associate with this sport (people, verbs and things).
player

2 🎥 Watch the video. Do they like the same players?

3 Watch again. Which Key phrase is not in the dialogue?

4 Complete the dialogue with the Key phrases. Watch again and check.

Carmel
Did you see the football last night?

Louis
Yes, with the best player in the world. Mo Salah!

Carmel
Salah! There are lots of other good players. **1** (…) Firmino?

Louis
OK. You've got a point – Firmino's pretty good. Who else?

Carmel
Mbappé for example, he played well yesterday. **2** (…) there are lots of good French players.

Louis
Yes, I think you're **3** (…) .

Carmel
And what do you think of Kanté? **4** (…) , Kanté is better than Salah.

Louis
OK – Kanté is good, the French team is good, and Firmino's good. But there's still only one great player. The superstar. The best in the world. The Egyptian King – Salaaaaaah!

Carmel
5 (…)

5 Create your own dialogue. Follow the steps in the Skills boost.

SKILLS BOOST

THINK
Think about your favourite singers or sports people. Make notes about them.

PREPARE
Prepare a dialogue. Remember to include phrases for asking about and expressing opinions.

PRACTISE
Practise your dialogue.

PERFORM
Act out your dialogue for the class.

6 **Peer review** Listen to your classmates and answer the questions.
1 Who do they talk about?
2 Which Key phrases do they use to express opinions?
3 Do you agree with their opinions?

Key phrases
Asking for opinions: What do you think of … ?
What about … ?
Giving opinions: I (don't) think …
If you ask me, …
Agreeing: Yes, I think you're right about that.
You've got a point.
Disagreeing: No way!
That's ridiculous.

Real-world grammar
Did you **see** the football last night?
He **played** well yesterday.

Phrasebook → p125

91

7 Writing

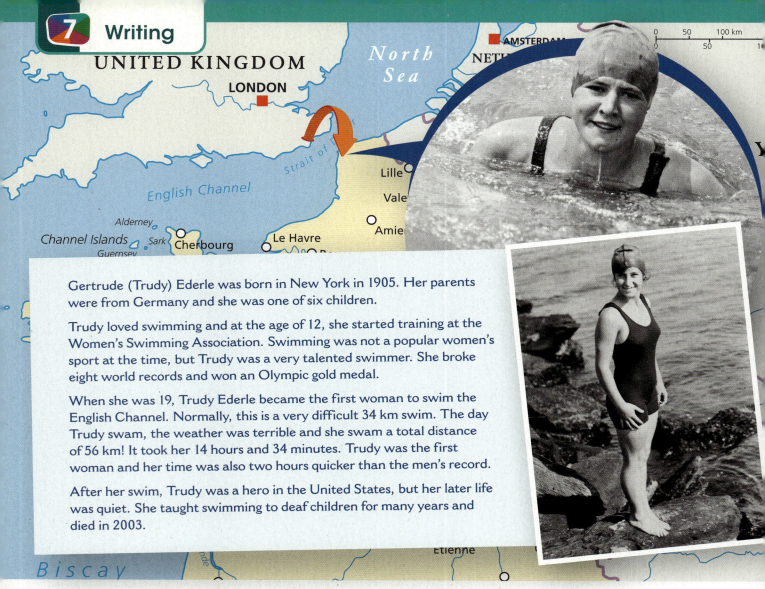

Gertrude (Trudy) Ederle was born in New York in 1905. Her parents were from Germany and she was one of six children.

Trudy loved swimming and at the age of 12, she started training at the Women's Swimming Association. Swimming was not a popular women's sport at the time, but Trudy was a very talented swimmer. She broke eight world records and won an Olympic gold medal.

When she was 19, Trudy Ederle became the first woman to swim the English Channel. Normally, this is a very difficult 34 km swim. The day Trudy swam, the weather was terrible and she swam a total distance of 56 km! It took her 14 hours and 34 minutes. Trudy was the first woman and her time was also two hours quicker than the men's record.

After her swim, Trudy was a hero in the United States, but her later life was quiet. She taught swimming to deaf children for many years and died in 2003.

A biography

1 Read the biography and choose the best title.
   a The longest swim
   b A sporting hero
   c Trudy loved swimming

2 Answer the questions.
   1 Where was Trudy born?
   2 How many brothers and sisters did she have?
   3 Did a lot of girls swim at that time?
   4 How do we know she was a talented swimmer?
   5 Why was Trudy's Channel swim difficult?
   6 How many extra kilometres did Trudy swim?
   7 Did the men swim faster than Trudy?
   8 What was Trudy's connection with swimming later in her life?

▶ **Subskill: Writing in paragraphs**
To help the reader understand, organise your writing into paragraphs. Each paragraph gives different information about the person.

3 Read descriptions a–f and choose the best one for each paragraph in the text. There are two you don't need.
   a Trudy at the Olympics
   b What Trudy did later
   c Trudy's swimming talent
   d Trudy's family
   e Trudy's Channel swim
   f When Trudy learnt to swim

4 Read the text and complete these time expressions we use when describing actions in the past. Write one word in each space.
   1 (…) 1905
   2 (…) (…) (…) (…) 12
   3 (…) (…) (…) 19
   4 (…) her swim

5 Use some of the expressions in exercise 4 to write three true sentences about yourself.

I moved to Mexico at the age of five.

6 Write a biography of a person from history you admire. Follow the steps in the Skills boost.

SKILLS BOOST

THINK
1 Choose a person.
2 Use the Internet to make notes about their life and what they did. Remember to check the information on more than one webpage.

> New York – 1905 – Germany – 6 children
> 12: WSA – swimming not popular
> 8 world records, Olympic gold

PREPARE
Organise your notes into logical paragraphs. For example:
- early life and family
- how they got started
- most important things they did
- later life

WRITE
Write your biography. Use the example in exercise 1 to help you.

… was born in …

CHECK
Read your biography. Answer the questions.
1 Do you include interesting information about the person?
2 Do you use past simple verbs correctly?
3 Do you use past time expressions?
4 Is your writing organised into logical paragraphs?

7 **Peer review** Exchange your biography with other students. Answer the questions.
1 Does the writer use past tenses and past time expressions?
2 What is the purpose of each paragraph?
3 Is it an interesting biography?

QUICK REVIEW 7

Grammar

Past simple
Regular and irregular verbs
Some verbs are regular in the past simple. They normally add -ed.
*She **started** school at nine o'clock.*
Other verbs are irregular and have different forms and spelling.
*He **had** lunch at 12:30.*

Common irregular verbs include:
come → came   do → did
give → gave   go → went
have → had   see → saw

For a fuller list of irregular verbs, see pp126–127.

Negative and question forms
Form the negative: *didn't* (*did not*) + infinitive
*They **didn't do** their homework.*
Form *Yes/No* questions: *Did* (*you*) + infinitive?
Form short answers: *Yes, (I) did./No, (I) didn't.*
***Did** you **understand** the exercise?*   *Yes, I **did**.*
***Did** she **have** dinner with her family last night?*   *No, she **didn't**.*

Past time expressions
Use time expressions to refer to the past:
*five years **ago***
***in** (2010)*
***when I was** eight*
***at the age of** nine*

Vocabulary

🔊 47 **Jobs**
accountant, actor, artist, businessman, businesswoman, chef, dentist, doctor, engineer, journalist, lawyer, manager, mechanic, nurse, photographer, pilot, police officer, receptionist, sales assistant, scientist, singer, taxi driver, teacher, waiter, web designer

🔊 48 **Adjectives to describe people**
careful, careless, friendly, generous, kind, lazy, normal, polite, rude, special, talented, unfriendly, unkind

93

Project

What makes a hero?

TASK: Make a digital presentation about a hero from the past.

Learning outcomes
1 I can talk about a hero and say why they are important.
2 I can be responsible for my learning.
3 I can use appropriate language from the unit.

Graphic organiser → Project planner p121

1 ▶ Watch a video of a student giving a presentation about a hero from the past. Why is Katherine Johnson a hero?

STEP 1: THINK ◼◻◻◻

2 Read the slides in the Model project. Which questions do they answer?
 1 Why is she a hero?
 2 What was her job?
 3 When was she born?
 4 Who were the other people in her family?
 5 What did she do?

3 Which of these things can you see?
 • pictures
 • questions
 • long sentences
 • facts and dates

STEP 2: PLAN ◼◼◻◻

4 Work in pairs. Make a list of heroes. Think about people in science, sports, politics, literature, music, etc.

5 Individually, choose a hero. Make notes for your presentation. Use the presentation slides to help you.

STEP 3: CREATE ◼◼◼◻

6 Read the *How to …* tips on p121. Then create your digital presentation.
 1 Give general information – who is this person? What did they do?
 2 Give information about their early life.
 3 Give information about their job/activities.
 4 Say why you think they are a hero.

7 Work in pairs. Read the tips in the Super skills box and practise saying the Key phrases with a partner.

CREATIVITY

Using feedback to improve your work

Tips
Ask other students to help you.
Listen to their suggestions.
Change your work to make it better.

Key phrases
I really like the part about …
How about including … ?
Why don't you … ?
This part is really clear.
What do you think about … ?
I didn't really understand …

8 Practise your presentation in groups. Use the tips and Key phrases in the Super skills box. What changes do other students suggest you make?

Model project

My hero from the past

1 Katherine Johnson
- a maths genius and scientist – 'the human computer'
- worked at NASA
- helped to send people into space

2 Her early life
- 1918 – born in West Virginia in the USA
- 1928 – started high school
- went to university – studied maths and French
- became a teacher

3 Her work
- 1953 – started work at NASA
- helped to send the first American into space
- helped to send Apollo 11 to the Moon

4 Why is she a hero?
- 'Girls are capable of doing everything men are capable of doing.'

STEP 4: PRESENT

9 Present your digital presentation to the class.

10 **Peer review** As you listen to your classmates, answer the questions.
1 Is the presentation clear and interesting?
2 Who is the most important hero from the past?

7 FINAL REFLECTION

1 The task
How well can you talk about the life of a hero from the past?
How well can you give a digital presentation?

2 Super skill
Can you listen to suggestions from your classmates and make changes? Give examples.

3 Language
Do you use language from the unit? Give examples.

8 Summer fun

WDYT? (What do you think?)

What's your idea of a good holiday?

Vocabulary: holidays; holiday activities

Grammar: *will* for predictions; future with *going to*; present continuous for future arrangements

Reading: a travel blog about Virtual Reality holidays

Listening: phone conversations and messages about holiday plans

Speaking: making arrangements

Writing: invitations

Project: create a three-day holiday plan for you and your friends

Video skills p97

Real-world speaking p103

Project pp106–107

96

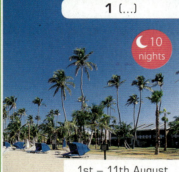
1 (...) 10 nights
1st – 11th August
Have fun in the sun

2 (...) 6 nights
13th – 19th January
It's the season for snow

3 (...) 5 nights
24th – 29th June
Sleep under the stars

Holidays

1 Look at the travel website. Match the types of holidays in the box with photos 1–7.

> go **camping**   go on a **city break**   go on a **walking holiday**
> go on a **water sports holiday**   go **skiing**
> go to a **theme park resort**   go to the **beach**

2 Work in pairs. Tell your partner about your favourite and least favourite type of holiday. Explain why.

3 Match the sentences with the places in the box.

> apartment   B & B   campsite
> country cottage   hotel   youth hostel

1 A really good one has five stars.
2 The letters in this name stand for 'Bed and Breakfast'.
3 If you stay here, you don't sleep in a bed or in a building.
4 This is a small house. It isn't in the town.
5 This place is only for you and your family. You can cook your own food there.
6 Here there are often a lot of beds in one room.

4 For each holiday type in exercise 1, say one or more places to stay.

Vocabulary 8

4 (...)
3 nights
3rd – 6th March
Culture and shopping

5 (...)
7 nights
12th – 19th May
Put your boots on

6 (...)
2 nights
18th – 20th April
THE WORLD'S BEST RIDES

7 (...)
5 nights
4th – 9th July
Splash!

7 Read the descriptions and complete with places to stay and facilities.

1 Last year we went camping at a (...) on Koh Kam Nui. There isn't a (...), but that isn't important because it's right next to the beach.
2 My cousin's wedding was in a small (...) in Monteverde. It was a sunny day and they got married in the (...).
3 When we went to Prague on a city break we stayed in an (...) so we could make our own food. They offered (...) so we had a cheap way to travel round the city.
4 Last summer we went on a walking holiday near Banff and we stayed in a (...) with six people in each room because it was cheap. There wasn't a TV, but there was a (...) where you could play table tennis.

8 💬 Complete your own dream holiday form and tell your partner about it.

My dream holiday	
Type	city break in New York City
Place	5-star hotel
Facilities	swimming pool with jacuzzi, big games room

5 💬 Work in pairs. Discuss the places you stay in when you go on holiday.

Where do you stay?

We usually stay in an apartment at the beach.

6 Match the facilities in the box to icons 1–7.

bike hire   car park   games room   garden
gym   picnic area   swimming pool

VIDEO SKILLS

9 🎥 Watch the video. What different holidays do you see?

10 💬 Work in pairs. Discuss the questions.
1 What is the main reason for this video?
   a to see the vlogger's holiday photos
   b to hear about different people's holidays
   c to sell a holiday
2 Who do you think would like this video?
3 What makes the video interesting? Think about: colours, photos, 360° effect, the presenter.

8 Reading and critical thinking

A travel blog

1 💬 **Work in pairs. Read the holiday facts and discuss the questions.**
1 What type of holiday can you have in each place?
2 What facilities can you expect?
3 Which of the places would you most like to visit and why?

Holiday facts

The world's most popular theme park is **The Magic Kingdom at Walt Disney World in Florida**, with more than an estimated 20 million visitors a year.

The world's most expensive hotel room is in **Geneva, Switzerland**. It costs around $80,000 a night!

The world's first space tourist paid $20 million to visit the **International Space Station**.

2 💬 **Work in pairs. Look at the photos on p99 and answer the questions.**
1 What can you see in the photos?
2 What connects them?

3 Read the introduction and the first paragraph of the text. Check your answers in exercise 2.

4 🔊 49 Read and listen to the text and choose the best summary.
a There are lots of problems with traditional holidays.
b Virtual Reality will change how people buy and experience travel.
c People will stop travelling when we have Virtual Reality.

5 Are the sentences true or false? Find information in the text to support your answer.
1 In the future, people will experience different places cheaply.
2 A travel company is using VR as an alternative holiday.
3 You can wear VR glasses in the sea when swimming with dolphins.
4 People sitting in the same room will have the same VR experience.
5 A grandmother takes VR holidays because she has problems walking.

▶ **Subskill: Identifying facts and opinions**
When you read, be careful to recognise the difference between fact and opinion. Adjectives like *amazing* and *terrible* and phrases like *I think* often indicate a personal opinion.

6 Find the information in the text. Which sentences are fact and which are opinion?
1 Virtual Reality travel is amazing.
2 A travel company now offers customers the chance to see their hotel using VR.
3 Special VR clothes help people feel as well as see.
4 VR shoes are fantastic.
5 A woman uses VR to visit destinations a long way from home.
6 VR glasses cost about $400.
7 VR glasses will get cheaper.

7 **Word work** Match the definitions to the words in bold in the text.
1 a large piece of material you use when jumping out of a plane
2 a place where water comes down from a high place
3 a very bad situation
4 a document you need for travelling to other countries
5 reserve (e.g. a restaurant or hotel)
6 walk up a hill or mountain

8 Complete the sentences with words from exercise 7.
1 You (…) 327 steps to the top of the building.
2 We didn't (…) the restaurant and when we arrived there weren't any free tables.
3 I lost my (…) and had to go to the police station.
4 Last year we visited the (…) in the Iguazu National Park.
5 I'm really frightened of flying, so the idea of a (…) jump is a complete (…) for me.

CRITICAL THINKING

1 **Remember** Look at the text. Which advantages of Virtual Reality travel does it mention?
2 **Evaluate** Put the advantages in order of importance in your opinion.
3 What disadvantages can you see of VR holidays? Write a list.
4 Would you like to go on a Virtual Reality holiday? Why/Why not?
5 **Create** Think of another activity that would be good to experience using Virtual Reality. Explain why.

Home | Activities | Guide | FAQ | About us | Contact us

Sit back, get comfortable and … TRAVEL?

This week on THE HOLIDAY BLOG, I'm looking at how Virtual Reality (VR) could change all our ideas about holidays.

Would you like to `climb` Mount Everest? How about staying in a 5-star hotel or going skiing in New Zealand? If, like me, your answer is 'Yes, but…', don't worry. You will soon be able to do all this and it won't cost a lot of money. How? With amazing VR travel.

With VR, some of the things that can turn your perfect holiday into a `nightmare` simply disappear. One travel company recently started offering customers a virtual tour of their hotel. Can you see the swimming pool from your room? What's the games room like? Put on your VR glasses and take a look before you `book`.

With VR you can swim with dolphins, or take a `parachute` jump while the person next to you visits a `waterfall`. And soon the experience will be even better with special clothes to wear during your VR trip. With your VR shoes you will be able to see the water and feel the sea on your feet. Fantastic!

You don't need a `passport` or sun cream, just your VR glasses. See you in Bali, or Alaska, or …

 The Holiday Guy   Comments (5)   10 Likes   Share

COMMENTS

 Lucien posted 14 June 11:42 am
For me, food is the most important thing about a holiday. With VR you can visit Italy, but you can't eat pizza!

 The Holiday Guy posted 14 June 11:55 am
Good point, Lucien. But I'm sure we will eat VR food in the future!

 Lucy Lake posted 15 June 3:33 pm
VR travel is also good for people who can't walk well. I read about an 80-year-old grandmother who takes 3D holidays in Egypt, India and Australia.

 Ryan posted 15 June 6:16 pm
What will this cost? Will it be expensive?

 The Holiday Guy posted 15 June 6:33 pm
No, it won't! VR glasses cost about $400 and I'm sure they'll get cheaper soon.

The longer read → Resource centre

8 Grammar

will for predictions: affirmative and negative

1 Copy and complete the table with the examples.

> We will eat VR food in the future.
> It won't cost a lot of money.

Affirmative and negative			
subject	will/won't	verb	
People	will	have	holidays in space.
1 (…)	(…)	(…)	(…)
We	won't	need	a passport.
2 (…)	(…)	(…)	(…)

2 Complete the predictions about holidays with the affirmative or negative form of the verb in brackets.

Ten years from now, …
1 people (…) (**have +**) holidays on the Moon.
2 we (…) (**need -**) passports. We (…) (**have +**) an ID microchip.
3 we (…) (**take -**) money on holiday. We (…) (**use +**) virtual money.
4 we (…) (**use +**) our phones to translate what people say when we're on holiday.

will for predictions: questions and short answers

3 Copy and complete the tables with the examples.

> What will this cost?
> Will it be expensive? No, it won't.

Questions	Short answers
Will we visit the Moon?	Yes, we will.
1 (…)	2 (…)

Wh- questions			
Question word	will	subject	verb
Where	will	we	travel?
3 (…)	(…)	(…)	(…)

4 💬 Work in pairs. Read the predictions in exercise 2 again. Do you agree with them?

> Will people have holidays on the Moon?
>
> No, they won't. Not in ten years.

5 Order the words to make questions.
1 speak to next / Who / on the phone / will / you ?
2 be like / tomorrow / What / the weather / will ?
3 you / go / tonight / What time / will / to bed ?
4 when you / What job / leave school / will / have / you ?

6 💬 Work in pairs. Ask and answer the questions in exercise 5.

7 Complete the text with the correct form of the verbs in the box.

> become   have   look   take   travel (x2)

How will holidays change in the future?

2030 According to a recent report, underwater hotels 1 (…) (+) more popular, but if you don't like that idea, your computer 2 (…) (+) at your online activity and suggest places to visit.

2050 Flying will be very different: aeroplanes 3 (…) (+) 360° windows. One question many people want to know is: 4 (…) (**we/?**) in space? The answer is yes, but not only to visit other planets. Planes will fly much higher and it 5 (…) (-) more than two and a half hours to fly from London to Sydney.

2100 Holidays will certainly be very different, but 6 (…) (**we/how/?**) Forget trains, planes and cars: Mary Jacquiline Romero, an expert from the University of Glasgow, predicts we will travel by teleportation!

8 Answer the question to solve the Brain teaser.

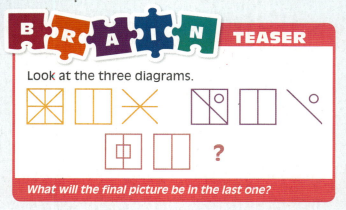

What will the final picture be in the last one?

Pronunciation: will → p117

Holiday activities

1 Read the blog. What activities can you see in the pictures?

Awesome things to do in the holidays!

In this week's blog, we look at some great ways to spend a 'staycation'.

1 Be a tourist at home
Perhaps you can't go on holiday, but you can be a tourist in your town. **Go sightseeing** and visit places of interest. **Go on a bus tour** or just walk around.

2 Get wet!
Spend a day at the swimming pool or **go to a water park**. Better still, **go on a day trip** to the beach and swim in the sea.

3 Spend time outside
Go for a bike ride every day or **go for a walk** in the park. When it's sunny, take a book or music and **sunbathe**. Don't forget your sunglasses!

4 Make mealtimes special
Go for a pizza with friends at a local pizzeria or invite them to your house and **have a barbecue** at home.

5 Enjoy the arts
Find out what's on in your town in the holidays. **Visit a museum or an art gallery**. If you prefer live music, **go to a concert**.

6 Help out
Don't just **hang out with friends** all summer, do something useful. Volunteer for a local charity or offer to **look after** neighbours' **pets**.

7 Organise visits
Take time to **visit family** – aunts, uncles and cousins. Arrange to **stay with a friend** or invite them to stay with you.

2 Match the definitions to some of the phrases in bold in the blog.
1 eat pizza in a restaurant
2 visit a place for a day
3 spend time with friends
4 visit interesting places in a town or city
5 sleep at a friend's house
6 walk for fun
7 lie in the sun

Vocabulary and Listening 8

3 Complete the phrases with the correct words from the blog.
1 (…) a bus tour/a day trip
2 (…) a water park/a concert
3 (…) a bike ride/a walk/a pizza

4 💬 Work in pairs. What do you think are the three best ideas in the blog? Why?

Phone conversations and messages

5 🔊 50 Listen to six people expressing how they're feeling. Match the words in the box to the speakers.

| bored confused excited nervous sad surprised |

▶ **Subskill: Listening for feelings**
To identify a speaker's feelings, listen to words and intonation.

6 🔊 51 Listen to three speakers on the phone. How is each speaker feeling?
a Sam   b Nina   c Ed

7 Listen again. In which extract does a speaker talk about a plan to … ?
1 go for a walk
2 go to a water park
3 look after a younger sister
4 hang out with a friend
5 meet at the weekend

8 Listen again and answer the questions.
1 When and where do Sam and Alisha plan to meet?
2 When is the music festival?
3 When does Lily plan to buy tickets?
4 When does Ed want to meet his friend?
5 What two activities does he say that they can do?

9 💬 Work in pairs. Answer the questions.
1 How long are the school holidays in your country? (How many weeks?)
2 Do you ever feel bored in the summer holidays? Why/Why not?
3 What do you think is the ideal number of weeks for the summer holiday?

8 Grammar

Future with *going to*

1 Read the examples and complete the rule.

Affirmative
I'm going to buy tickets tomorrow.
She's going to look after her sister.
They're going to try the new water slide.
Negative
I'm not going to have a holiday this year.
He isn't going to see his friends.
They aren't going to be home until late.

To talk about future plans and intentions, use:
subject + (…) (*not*) + *going to* + (…) .

2 Complete the sentences with *going to* and the verb in brackets.
1 I (…) **(study)** for exams next weekend.
2 My mum (…) **(not work)** on Saturday.
3 My parents (…) **(go)** shopping.
4 A friend (…) **(come)** to my place to play games.
5 I (…) **(not watch)** TV.

3 Change the sentences in exercise 2 to make them true for you about next weekend.
I'm not going to study for exams next weekend. I'm going to hang out with friends.

4 Copy and complete the table with *is*, *are*, *isn't* or *aren't*.

Questions	Short answers
Are you going to be at home this afternoon?	Yes, I am. No, I'm not.
1 (…) she going to go to the concert?	Yes, she is. No, she 2 (…) .
3 (…) they going to play games?	Yes, they are. No, they 4 (…) .

5 Order the words to make questions.
1 holiday / go / going / on / Are / this summer / you / to ?
2 going / Where / to / you / go / are ?
3 stay / to / are / you / Where / going ?
4 to / you / going / on / go / Are / any day trips ?

6 💬 Work in pairs. Ask and answer the questions in exercise 5. What did you learn about your partner's summer plans?

Present continuous for future arrangements

7 Read the examples and choose the correct option in the rule.

We're meeting at the bus station at 8:00.
A band is playing in the park on Saturday.
What are you doing this afternoon?

We use the present continuous to talk about **possible**/**definite** arrangements in the future.

8 Read Marco's calendar and write sentences about his plans for the week.

Monday	meet Liam 1:00
Tuesday	have a guitar lesson 5:30
Wednesday	get a bus to the water park 8:00
Thursday	go to the cinema with Izan 7:00
Friday	stay with Adrian
Saturday	travel to the mountains

On Monday, he's meeting Liam at one o'clock.

9 Choose the correct option.

GRAMMAR ROUND-UP
1 2 3 4 5 6 7 8

Why not try geocaching this summer?

I **1 discover/'m discovering/discovered** geocaching two years **2 before/ago/past**. The idea is simple. You go to the geocaching website, and it **3 give/is giving/gives** you the location of a box. You use the GPS on your phone to find it.

There **4 is/are/was** objects in the box. You take one, but you **5 can/can't/must** put another object back into the box – those are the rules of the game!

The last time I went geocaching, for example, there **6 is/was/were** a key ring. I **7 take/'m taking/took** it and put in some pens.

This summer, I **8 will/going to/'m going to** do it again. I love being in the countryside, and this is **9 good/better/best** than going for a walk. Try it, you **10 love/are loving/will love** it!

Research

Where can you go geocaching in your country?

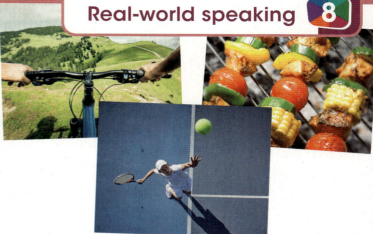

Real-world speaking 8

Making arrangements

1 Work in pairs. Talk about your plans for next weekend.

2 📹 Watch the video and answer the questions.
  1. What do Maria and Sam decide to do?
  2. When and where are they going to meet?

3 Watch again. Which Key phrases do you hear?

4 Complete the dialogue with the Key phrases. Watch again and check.

Maria: Hey, why don't we go for a bike ride this weekend?
Sam: Great idea! When?
Maria: How about Saturday morning?
Sam: 1 (…) Saturday morning. I'm going to the dentist.
Maria: Poor you! 2 (…) in the afternoon?
Sam: 3 (…) , I'm going to help my dad. We're having a barbecue to celebrate my exam results. 4 (…) anything Sunday?
Maria: I'm playing tennis in the morning, but 5 (…) in the afternoon.
Sam: Me, too.
Maria: OK, let's meet at the park at 2:30.
Sam: Awesome!

5 Create your own dialogue. Follow the steps in the Skills boost.

SKILLS BOOST

THINK
Individually, make a diary of a week. Write activities in the diary. Leave two days free.

PREPARE
Prepare a dialogue. Choose an activity you both want to do, and decide when you can do it.

PRACTISE
Practise your dialogue.

PERFORM
Act out your dialogue for the class.

6 **Peer review** Listen to your classmates and answer the questions.
  1. What do they decide to do and when do they decide to do it?
  2. How many Key phrases do they use?

Key phrases
What are you doing Saturday?
What are you up to Saturday?
Nothing special. Why?
I can't Saturday morning. I'm …
Are you free in the afternoon?
How about Saturday morning?
Yes, I think so. / No, sorry, I'm …
Are you doing anything Sunday?
I'm busy Sunday morning.
I'm free in the afternoon.

 **US → UK**

How about Saturday morning? (US) → How about *on* Saturday morning? (UK)

Let's meet at *two thirty*. (US) → Let's meet at *half past two*. (UK)

8 Writing

Invitations

1 Match the emojis with the meanings.

| a party | Bye! | camping | happy | sad | bike |

2 Read the messages. Who is going … ?
1 camping at the weekend
2 for a bike ride on Monday

3 Answer the questions.
1 When is Ian leaving to go camping?
2 Why can't Emma go for a bike ride on Monday afternoon?
3 What time is Jake meeting Emma?
4 Where are they meeting?
5 What is Jake doing on Sunday?

4 Read the messages again. Find three phrases for inviting and four phrases for responding yes or no.

Inviting	Responding ('yes')	Responding ('no')
Do you want to go for a bike ride on Monday afternoon?		

5 Complete the messages with phrases for inviting and responding.

Hi, Josh! Do 1 (…) going to the cinema?

I 2 (…) to. When?

On Saturday evening.

Sorry, 3 (…). I'm going for a 🍕 with Sean and Becky. Would you 4 (…) come?

OK, 5 (…) fun.

▶ **Subskill: Apostrophes**

We use apostrophes to show possession (*my mum's car*) or with contractions (*That's (is) great!*).

6 Find examples of apostrophes in the messages on p104 …
  a with a singular noun to show possession
  b with a plural noun to show possession
  c to substitute a letter or letters in a word (contraction)

7 Add the missing apostrophes in each sentence.
  1 Its hot today so Im going to the park.
  2 Id love to come, but Ive got a guitar lesson.
  3 Sorry, we cant. Were going for a pizza to celebrate Pauls birthday.
  4 My parents anniversary is on Saturday and theyre having a party.

8 Write a message dialogue. Follow the steps in the Skills boost.

> **SKILLS BOOST**
>
> **THINK**
> 1 Think of a place you want to go to, or an activity you want to do.
> 2 Choose a day and a time to do this.
>
> **PREPARE**
> Make notes for your messages. Include an invitation (Person A) and a reply to the invitation (Person B)
>
> | Person A | Person B |
> |---|---|
> | 1 Ask about plans | 2 Say you aren't sure |
> | 3 Make an invitation | 4 Say 'no', and why |
> | 5 Make a second invitation | 6 Say 'yes' |
> | 7 Arrange where and when to meet | |
>
> **WRITE**
> Write your message dialogue.
>
> **CHECK**
> Read your messages. Answer the questions.
> 1 Do you use *going to* for plans/intentions, and the present continuous for future arrangements?
> 2 Do you use phrases for inviting and replying?
> 3 Do you use apostrophes correctly?

9 **Peer review** Exchange your messages with another student. Answer the questions.
  1 What does the writer decide to do and when?
  2 Which phrases does the writer use to invite and respond to an invitation?
  3 Does the writer use apostrophes correctly?

QUICK REVIEW 8

Grammar

will for predictions
To make predictions about the future, use: *will/won't* + infinitive without *to*
Aeroplanes **will be** bigger and faster.
People **won't travel** by train or car.
To make questions, use: (Question word) + *will* + subject + infinitive without *to*
Will people **go** on holiday in 2050? Yes, they **will**./No, they **won't**.
What **will** it **cost**?

Future with *going to*
To talk about future plans and intentions, use *going to*.
subject + *be* (*not*) + *going to* + infinitive
Nina **isn't going to go** to the concert.
They**'re going to meet** and play games.
To make questions with *going to*, use:
(Question word) + *be* + subject + infinitive
What **are** you **going to do** this summer?
Are you **going to go** on holiday? Yes, I **am**./No, I**'m not**.

Present continuous for future arrangements
To talk about future arrangements, use the present continuous.
We**'re meeting** at the bus station at 8:00.
We **aren't going** on holiday this year.
What **are** you **doing** on Saturday?

Vocabulary

🔊 52 **Types of holiday**
go camping, go on a city break, go on a walking holiday, go on a water sports holiday, go skiing, go to a theme park resort, go to the beach

🔊 53 **Places to stay**
apartment, B & B, campsite, country cottage, hotel, youth hostel

🔊 54 **Facilities**
bike hire, car park, games room, garden, gym, picnic area, swimming pool

🔊 55 **Holiday activities**
go for a bike ride, go for a pizza, go for a walk, go on a bus tour, go on a day trip, go sightseeing, go to a concert, go to a water park, hang out with friends, have a barbecue, look after a pet, stay with a friend, sunbathe, visit a museum or art gallery, visit family

105

8 Project

What's your idea of a good holiday?

TASK: Create a three-day holiday plan for you and your friends.

Learning outcomes
1 I can plan a trip and present ideas clearly.
2 I can communicate my opinions in a group discussion.
3 I can use appropriate language from the unit.

Graphic organiser → Project planner p121

1 Watch a video of students practising their holiday plan presentation. Where do they want to go?

STEP 1: THINK

2 Look at the holiday plan in the Model project. What information does it include?
- how much things cost
- exact time of activities
- type of accommodation
- ideas for meals
- plans for activities and places to visit
- things to pack

3 Would you like to go on this trip? Why/Why not?

STEP 2: PLAN

4 Work in groups. Read the tips in the Super skills box and practise saying the Key phrases with your group.

COMMUNICATION

Communicating clearly

Tips
Look at your classmates when you speak.
When you give an opinion, give reasons why.
Make sure all your classmates agree.
Make sure everyone participates fully in the discussion.

Key phrases
I think this is a good idea because …
Do we all agree?
You're very quiet. What do you think?
What do you think is best?
I think this is the best option because …
I don't think that's a good idea because …

5 Work in groups of three. Choose a place to visit for a three-day holiday. Use the tips and Key phrases in the Super skills box. Consider:
- the type of accommodation you can stay in
- places to visit and activities you can do there; include at least one cultural activity and one outdoor activity
- a mix of places that are interesting for everyone in the group
- different types of food for different meals
- a trip that won't be too expensive

STEP 3: CREATE

6 Choose a format and create your presentation.

7 Agree how you are going to present your plan. Read the *How to …* tips on p121 and practise your presentation.

Grammar and Vocabulary → Quick review p105

Model project

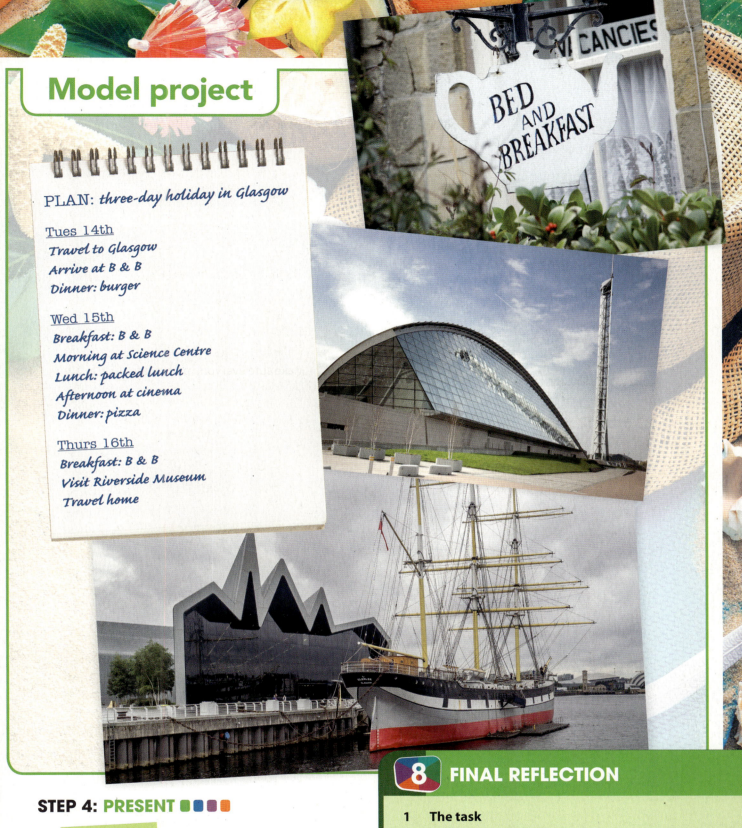

PLAN: three-day holiday in Glasgow

Tues 14th
Travel to Glasgow
Arrive at B & B
Dinner: burger

Wed 15th
Breakfast: B & B
Morning at Science Centre
Lunch: packed lunch
Afternoon at cinema
Dinner: pizza

Thurs 16th
Breakfast: B & B
Visit Riverside Museum
Travel home

STEP 4: PRESENT

8 **Peer review** Present your plan to another group. As you listen to your classmates, think about the questions.
1 Would you like to go on this holiday?
2 Is the information presented well?
3 Think of a question about the holiday plans.

8 FINAL REFLECTION

1 **The task**
Is the plan well prepared, with activities for different types of people?
Is the information clear and well presented?

2 **Super skill**
Does everyone communicate their ideas well in the group?

3 **Language**
Do you use language from the unit? Give examples.

9 Look what you know!

Vocabulary

1 Name the things you can see in the pictures.

2 For each word in exercise 1, write the letter indicated.

A	B	C	D	E	F	G	H	I
4th letter	5th letter	2nd letter	4th letter	3rd letter	2nd letter	1st letter	5th letter	1st letter
G								

3 Which word/phrase in each group does not go with the verb in bold?

1 **go**   home   to school   ~~football~~   skiing
2 **do**   your homework   sports   yoga   breakfast
3 **play**   in a band   gymnastics   hockey   a musical instrument
4 **start**   school at 8:00   a business   a new club   home
5 **go**   badminton   on a city break   sightseeing   to bed
6 **stay**   at home   sad   in a youth hostel   with a friend
7 **have**   a break   social media   a shower   a barbecue

4 Choose the correct verb for the odd one out in exercise 3.

play football

5 Work in pairs. Complete the questions using phrases from exercise 4. Then ask and answer.

1 When do you (…)?
2 Do you know anyone who (…)?
3 What time do you (…) after school?
4 Can you (…) at your school?
5 What do you do when you (…)?
6 How often do you (…)?

6 Match 1–12 with a–l to make compounds.

1	bus	a	bag
2	country	b	trip
3	day	c	cottage
4	games	d	cream
5	horse	e	driver
6	ice	f	park
7	department	g	pool
8	sleeping	h	riding
9	swimming	i	room
10	table	j	store
11	taxi	k	station
12	theme	l	tennis

7 Complete the description with words from exercise 6.

Last year I went on holiday with my cousins. We stayed in a **1** (…) in Devon. They had a **2** (…) where we could play **3** (…). There was also a **4** (…), but the water was really cold.

One day, we went on a **5** (…) to an amazing **6** (…). We all had a great time, but my cousin Finn ate too much **7** (…) and felt very bad on one of the rides!

I travelled home before my cousins. My aunt took me to the **8** (…), but at first we couldn't find it. In the end, a **9** (…) told us where to go.

I had a great holiday!

Look what you know! 9

Reading

1 Match 1–3 with a–c to make sentences. They give advice from the Subskills in Units 1–8.
1 Look at the title and pictures before you …
2 The first time you read a text, read quickly to get …
3 To find specific information, …

a underline key words in the question and look for similar words in the text.
b read to help you predict what is in the text.
c a general idea of what it's about.

> **Reading tip**
> Use the advice in exercise 1 to help you with the reading tasks on this page.

2 Look at the texts on this page but don't read them! Where are they from? How do you know?
a a live feed   b a book   c a newspaper

3 💬 Read the titles of the stories. With a partner predict three items of vocabulary you think are in each story.
a A place of extremes
b No more boys and girls
c Holiday essentials
d The best place to live

4 🔊 56 Read and listen to the stories. Match the titles in exercise 3 with each story.

5 Are the sentences true or false?
1 John Lewis stopped selling children's clothes.
2 One problem was the typical colour of girls' clothes.
3 Atacama is dry because of its position.
4 There's rain in all parts of the Atacama desert, but only a little.
5 Bristol is not a good place for cycling.
6 London isn't a very healthy city.
7 Over half of British people take food on holiday.
8 They take food because they can't ask for things in another language.

6 Correct the false sentences in exercise 5.

> **Exam tip**
> If a question has several parts, make sure you leave time to do all of them. If you don't try a question you won't get any points.

7 **Word work** The words in bold in the text all appeared in the Word work exercises in Units 1–8. Can you remember what they mean?

8 💬 Work in pairs. Order the stories from most to least interesting, then compare your order with your partner. If it's different, explain your reasons.

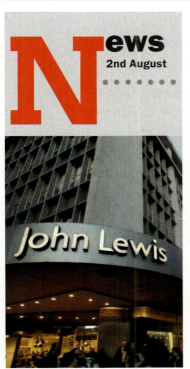

News
2nd August

1 (…)
Striped leggings, a top with dinosaurs, cool trainers – but are these great kids' clothes for boys or girls? At John Lewis department stores now, there isn't a difference. They didn't like the idea of pink clothes for girls, or boys' clothes with words like 'Future Scientist' so they decided to stop having separate sections for boys' and girls' clothes and just sell a **mix** of clothes for all children.

2 (…)
The Atacama in Chile is officially the driest **desert** on Earth. The **average** rainfall is just 1 mm and in parts of the desert, it never rains. Its position between the Andes mountains and the sea means that rain clouds often can't get to the Atacama. Experts think the last time it rained in some places was hundreds of years ago.

3 (…)
Britain's healthiest town is Bristol! With 45 sports clubs and more than 230 cycle routes, the **citizens** of Bristol live in the top place for a healthy life. Experts counted swimming pools, parks, sports centres and fast-food restaurants. What about London? It was number 5 – from the bottom!
Source: SBO.net

4 (…)
What do more than 60% of British people take when they go on holiday? Is it sun cream, a guidebook, or a toothbrush? You're wrong! The answer is quite strange! Among the things British people pack, one of the most important is food. Some people don't like foreign food and drinks; others think it's too expensive. Among the most popular things you can find in a British suitcase are tea and instant coffee, biscuits and noodles!

109

9 Look what you know!

Grammar

The questions round the edge of the page will help you remember the grammar studied in the book. First answer the red questions around the page. Next, do the exercises in the central red section. Then do the same with green, blue and yellow.

20 Complete the sentence: *When I get home from school later today, I (…) do my homework.*

The red sections focus on possessive adjectives and object pronouns, present simple, adverbs of frequency and *love, like, hate*.

1 Complete the sentences with a possessive adjective or object pronoun.
1 (you) Is that **your** pen?
2 (he) That's Alan. I sit with (…) in history.
3 (they) Oh – eggs! Sorry, I don't like (…) .
4 (she) Look at that girl! I love (…) jacket!
5 (we) Mr Anand is (…) maths teacher.
6 (we) Joel lives in the same street as (…) .
7 (I) Can you help (…) , please?

2 Choose the correct option.
1 My brother **studies/study** computer science.
2 Where **does/do** your grandparents live?
3 My dad **don't/doesn't** work in an office.
4 Do you like **play/playing** computer games?
5 We never **watch/watches** TV.
6 My brother **is always/always is** late for class.
7 I sometimes **listen/listening** to music.

3 Complete the sentences with the words in brackets.
1 A: What languages (…) **(you/speak)**?
   B: I (…) **(speak)** Turkish and a little German.
2 A: (…) **(your brother/do)** any sports?
   B: Yes, he (…) **(do)**. He (…) **(go)** swimming.
3 A: What hobbies (…) **(your parents/have)**?
   B: My dad (…) **(take)** photos, but my mum (…) **(not have)** much free time.
4 A: What time (…) **(your sister/get up)**?
   B: At 6 am. She often (…) **(study)** before school.

19 How do you write this sentence in the past? *Einstein is a famous scientist.*

18 You mustn't be late! Is it OK to be late?

The green sections focus on the present continuous, comparatives and superlatives, and modals of obligation.

1 Write the verbs in the present simple or present continuous.
Ben: Hi Josh. What 1 (…) **(you/do)** at the moment?
Josh: I 2 (…) **(walk)** to the sports centre. I always 3 (…) **(play)** basketball on Mondays. What about you?
Ben: Dad 4 (…) **(make)** dinner and I 5 (…) **(help)** him.
Josh: 6 (…) **(your dad/always/cook)**?
Ben: Only when he 7 (…) **(get)** home early.

2 Complete the questions with the comparative or superlative adjectives. Then ask a partner.
1 What is the (…) **(easy)** school subject?
2 Which is (…) **(difficult)** to learn, English or Japanese?
3 What is the (…) **(big)** shop in your town?
4 What is the (…) **(bad)** programme on television? Why?
5 Which is (…) **(good)**, pizza or ice cream?

3 Complete the school rules with *can, can't, must* or *mustn't*. Which rules do you have in your school?
1 Listen when others are speaking.
   You must listen when others are speaking.
2 Don't use your mobile phone in class.
3 It's OK to write on the board.
4 Bring your books to class.
5 Don't chat in class.
6 It's OK to wear trainers.
7 No eating in the classroom.

17 What form of a verb do you use after *like, love* and *hate*?

16 Make two predictions about your life in 2035.

15 What is the difference between *How much … ?* and *How many … ?*

14 What is the superlative form of the adjective *hot*?

13 Do adverbs of frequency (*always, sometimes, never*) come before or after the verb *be*?

110

Look what you know! 9

1 Complete the list: me, you, (...), (...), it, (...), you, (...)

2 Complete the sentence: *Right now, I'm ...*

3 Add two more words in each category. Countable nouns: *tomatoes*, (...), (...). Uncountable nouns: *rice*, (...), (...).

4 What do you add to regular verbs to make the past simple?

5 Rewrite the sentence in the negative form: *He gets up at seven o'clock.*

6 *She's playing tennis.* What do we call this tense? When do we use it?

7 Choose the correct option: *There is/are three museums near my home.*

8 What is the past simple of these irregular verbs? *go, meet, see, come, write*

9 Order the words to make a question: *do / go / Where / they / to school ?*

10 Write the comparative form of these adjectives: *tall, interesting.* What's the rule?

11 Complete the sentence: *We haven't got (...) milk.*

12 What is the question? *We went to the cinema last night.*

The blue sections focus on countable and uncountable nouns, *there is/are, some, any, much, many* and the past simple form of *be*.

1 Correct the mistake in each sentence.
1. Would you like a apple or a banana?
2. There are any great shops in town.
3. Is there some library near here?
4. There isn't some chocolate in the cake.
5. Are there any ice cream in the fridge?
6. I usually have a sandwich and a milk for breakfast.

2 Write questions for these answers using *How much ... ?* or *How many ... ?*
1. I play two sports: hockey and tennis.
2. I've got £20 in my pocket.
3. I've got two sisters.
4. I usually spend an hour a day on homework.
5. I eat an apple and a banana every day.
6. I usually read a book every month.

3 Complete the dialogue with *was/wasn't, were/weren't, there was/wasn't, there were/weren't* or *was/were there*.

Jamie: Hey, why **1** (...) you late for class this morning?
Carla: I **2** (...) at Levi's birthday party last night.
Jamie: Oh, right. **3** (...) a lot of people there?
Carla: Yes, **4** (...), and **5** (...) music and dancing.
Jamie: **6** (...) any food?
Carla: No, **7** (...), but **8** (...) a cake.

The yellow sections focus on the past simple and look at future forms.

1 Rewrite the sentences in the affirmative, negative or question form.
1. He came to school by car today. (?)
   Did he come to school by car today?
2. I didn't go to bed early last night. (+)
3. Did she help you with your homework? (-)
4. They took a picnic with them. (?)
5. Did the class start at 9:00? (+)
6. He didn't phone me at the weekend. (?)
7. They gave me their address. (-)

2 Write questions for the answers about Angus's evening out.
1. He went to the cinema.
   What did Angus do last night?
2. He saw an adventure film.
3. He went with Kate.
4. It cost €8.
5. They sat in the front row.
6. It started at 7:30.

3 Choose the correct option.
1. **Will you go/Are you going** to the park after school?
2. **I'm going to buy/I'll buy** a new game this weekend.
3. People **will have/are having** holidays on Mars in 2050.
4. People **won't use/aren't using** money in the future.
5. We **aren't going to/won't** stay at home this summer.

111

9 Look what you know!

Listening

1 💬 **Work in pairs. Answer the questions.**

1 Where and when do you listen to music?
2 How do you listen (using a mobile phone, with headphones, etc.)?
3 Do you ever listen to podcasts? Which ones?
- science
- sports
- history
- other

2 Look at the podcasts. What is each one about? Write three words you expect to hear in each programme.

> **Remember**
> Use key words to help you understand.

Sports live | Teen talk | Natural science | Future world
Good cooking! | News update | Travel tips | Tech news

3 🔊 57 **Listen to the extracts. Which five podcasts do you hear? Write the order 1–5.**

4 Listen again. Answer the questions.
1 What ingredients do you need to make the chocolate cake?
2 Where will people have holidays in ten years' time?
3 What extreme weather happened last night?
4 What do the people do with their clothes?
5 What was special about the giant tortoise?

5 💬 **Work in pairs. Answer the questions.**
1 Which podcasts do you think are interesting? Why?
2 Which one would you choose to listen to?

6 Look at the photo. What can you see? What do you know about these events?

7 🔊 58 **Listen to a podcast about e-sports. Choose the correct answer (a–c).**

> **Exam tip**
> Take time to read the questions before you listen.

1 Why does the speaker think e-sports are real sports?
  a Players must run and do exercise.
  b It's important to eat healthy food.
  c Players practise to be good at the game.
2 Why did e-sports start?
  a Technology became better.
  b More people wanted to play video games.
  c It was possible to watch games online.
3 In what ways are e-sports more than a hobby?
  a Players spend millions of dollars on games.
  b Traditional football teams have got e-players.
  c There's a world organisation for e-sports.
4 What does he think about e-sports at school?
  a Schools will have e-sports teams in the future.
  b They're good for students who can't do traditional sports.
  c It's a good idea to have video games at sports day.
5 What is his opinion about the future of e-sports?
  a They will be more popular than traditional sports.
  b There will be more e-sports programmes on TV.
  c People won't play football, only video games.

8 Listen again and check your answers.

9 💬 **Work in pairs. Name one thing about e-sports that …**
- you already knew
- you didn't know before
- you were surprised about

Look what you know! 9

Real-world speaking

1 Works in pairs. Look at the photos.
1. What is the situation in each photo?
2. What other situations did you learn about on the Real-world speaking pages?

2 Copy and complete the table with the Key phrases in the box.

Key phrases
How much is it?
What time does it start?
Is there an underground station near here?
Are you free on Saturday?
What do you think of hip hop music?
Why don't we take a picnic?

Asking for information	Shopping for clothes	Making suggestions

Asking for directions	Giving opinions	Making arrangements

3 Add two more phrases in each category in the table.

4 Choose the correct option.

- I'd like to **1 find out/find** about the gym, please.
- Of course.
- Have you got a karate class?
- Yes, we have.
- What day is it **2 at/on**?
- Mondays, from 7 to 9.
- Can I **3 sign up/look** for it?
- Yes, of course.

- Can I **4 try/put** these trainers on, please?
- Sure.
- They look good, but they're a bit small.
- What **5 size/type** are they?
- 37. Have you got them in a 38?
- Yes, here you are.
- Oh, these are better. I'll **6 take/buy** them.

5 Work in pairs. Create a dialogue for one of these situations. Follow the steps in the Skills boost.

A Make an arrangement to do something together this weekend.
Discuss when you are free. You like different things, but decide what to do and when to do it.

B You're shopping. You want to buy a present for a friend's birthday.
Make suggestions about what to buy (you have different ideas). Make a decision and buy your present.

C Talk about a course or hobby that you started recently.
Ask and answer questions about where and when you do it. Talk about your first experience and respond with interest!

SKILLS BOOST

THINK
Choose a situation.

PREPARE
Write your dialogue. Include at least four Key phrases.

PRACTISE
Practise your dialogue. Try to remember it.

PERFORM
Act out your dialogue for the class.

Exam tip
Try to stay calm in speaking exams. Take deep breaths before you start.

6 **Peer review** Listen to your classmates and answer the questions.
1. Which task did they choose?
2. Which Key phrases did they use?

9 Look what you know!

Writing

1 Read the texts quickly. Match text types 1–5 with examples A–E.

1 a blog   2 an invitation   3 an email   4 instructions   5 a forum post

A Molly

Hi Molly,

How was your holiday? I went to the north of France. We stayed in a cottage and went walking every day. It was beautiful, but the weather wasn't good …

B First of all, draw a circle. ➡ Then add two circles for the eyes. ➡ Remember, in animé, the eyes are always big …

C HOME | ABOUT | BLOG | CONTACT

My Diary

Posted by Lee 13th June

This week our class did a project about animals. We could talk about endangered animals or animals that were extinct …

D
Hi! How are things?
Hi Abby!
Good, thanks. I'm going shopping this afternoon. Do you want to come?
Sure! Can Fran come too?

E Register | FAQ | New Posts | Community

What are the typical dishes in your country?

Hi, I'm from Italy. Italian food is famous all over the world because it's really good! Our most popular dishes are pasta (in my region we cook it with pesto, a green sauce) …

2 Find the words or phrases in the texts and answer the questions. You have five minutes!

1 *First of all, Then …*
   Write three more words to order events. **(Unit 6)**

2 two countries with capital letters
   Name four rules for capital letters. **(Unit 1)**

3 *and, but, or*
   Which do we use to add … ? **(Unit 2)**
   a a different idea
   b a similar idea
   c an alternative

4 an adjective to describe a place
   Write three other adjectives to describe places. **(Unit 5)**

5 *too*
   What other words do we use to add information? What is the position of these words in a sentence? **(Unit 4)**

6 *because*
   What is the difference between *because* and *so*? **(Unit 3)**

3 Correct the sentences.

1 I went swimming and I played volleyball also.
2 We have maths on mondays.
3 There are lots of interestings things to do here.
4 Do you prefer quiet and busy places?
5 We stayed in a town small in spain last august.

4 Choose one task and write your answer in 120 words. Follow the steps in the Skills boost.

A Write a blog about your last holiday.
Describe the weather, where you stayed and what you did. What was the best thing about the holiday?

B Write an email to a friend.
Tell him/her about plans for the end of the school year and the summer.

C You see this post online. Write your answer.
I want to visit new places, but I don't know where to go. Tell me about your town or city. What can I do there?

SKILLS BOOST

THINK
Make notes about the information to include.

PREPARE
Organise your writing into paragraphs.

WRITE
Write your blog, email or online post.

CHECK
Check your writing for tenses, vocabulary, punctuation and linking words (*so, because, but,* etc.).

5 **Peer review** Exchange your writing with other students. Answer the questions.

1 Which task did they do?
2 Are the tenses, vocabulary, punctuation and linking words correct?

Look what you know! 9

REVIEW GAME

How to play the REVIEW GAME
1. Form groups of three to five students.
2. Each student needs a different coin or marker. Put these on START.
3. In turn, roll a dice, move forward and do what it says on the square.
4. The winner is the first to FINISH!

Key phrases:
You start.
Whose turn is it?
What's the question?
It's your/my turn.

START

1 Ask someone in your group for directions to a place in your town.

2  Talk about what you eat on a typical day.

3 You have one minute. How many objects in the classroom can you name?

4 Miss a turn

5 Compare your city with another place in your country.

6  Describe what someone in your group is wearing.

7 Go back three squares

8 Make arrangements to meet someone in your group next weekend.

9 Talk about the rules in your ideal school.

10 Speak for one minute about 'My last birthday'.

11 Describe your typical day.

12 Go forward two squares

13 Tell the group about one of your heroes.

14  Speak for one minute about 'My favourite sport'.

15 Say what you did last weekend.

16 Say four things you can take on a trip.

17 Miss a turn

18 Speak for one minute about 'My plans for the holidays'.

19 Go back to START

20  You have one minute. How many animals can you name?

21  Describe the weather in your country at different times of the year.

FINISH

Pronunciation

Unit 1
Silent letters

Some words in English have silent letters: we write the letter but we do not say it.

1 🔊 59 Listen to the words. Which letters are not pronounced?
1. history
2. design
3. technology
4. literature
5. chemistry
6. geography

2 Find the silent letters in the words.
1. biscuit
2. camera
3. chocolate
4. cousin
5. cupboard
6. daughter
7. guitar
8. interesting
9. stationery
10. white

3 🔊 60 Listen and check. Repeat the words in exercise 2.

Unit 2
do you /djʊ/

1 🔊 61 Listen to the questions. Underline the stressed words.
1. What sport do you like?
2. When do you play?
3. Where do you play?
4. Who do you play with?
5. Why do you like this sport?

Pronunciation of do you

When the words *do you* aren't stressed in a question, we often pronounce them /djʊ/.

2 🔊 62 Listen and repeat /djʊ/.

3 Listen again and repeat the questions in exercise 1.

Unit 3
/n/ and /ŋ/

1 🔊 63 Listen and repeat the words with /n/.
trainers   sandals   clean   design

2 🔊 64 Listen and repeat the words with /ŋ/.
English   think   practising   singer

3 🔊 65 Listen to the words. Do you hear a or b?
1. a thin   b thing
2. a call in   b calling
3. a win   b wing
4. a go in   b going

4 🔊 66 Listen and repeat the tongue-twisters.
1. Lynne is wearing thin pink leggings.
2. I'm singing and Finn is playing the violin.

Unit 4
can

/kæn/ or /kən/?

In questions and affirmative sentences, *can* is not stressed, so we say /kən/.
In short answers, we say /kæn/.

1 🔊 67 Listen to the two pronunciations of *can*.
1 /kæn/   2 /kən/

2 Look at the dialogue. How do you say *can* in each case, /kən/ or /kæn/?

A: **1** Can I go shopping this afternoon?
B: Yes, you **2** can. You **3** can get some new trainers.
A: **4** Can Ellen come with me?
B: Yes, she **5** can. You **6** can go to that new fast-food restaurant.

3 🔊 68 Listen and check your answers in exercise 2. Work in pairs and practise the dialogue.

Pronunciation

Unit 5
/iː/ and /ɪ/

1 🔊 69 Listen and repeat the words with a long *i* sound /iː/.

> beef   cheese   peas   read   teach   we

2 🔊 70 Listen and repeat the words with a short *i* sound /ɪ/.

> bit   chips   gym   milk   physics   wind

3 Find the /iː/ and /ɪ/ sounds in the sentence.
Six teams are swimming in the freezing sea.

4 🔊 71 Listen to the words. Is the sound short or long?
1 eat
2 it
3 skin
4 minute
5 sheep
6 liquid

Unit 6
Past simple endings /d/ /t/ /ɪd/

Pronouncing -ed
There are three pronunciations of *-ed* endings: /d/ /t/ and /ɪd/.

1 🔊 72 Listen to the pronunciation of the verbs in the table.

/d/	/t/	/ɪd/
played	watched	visited

2 🔊 73 Copy the table in exercise 1. Listen and add the verbs in the box.

> finished   decided   helped   listened   needed
> received   started   stopped   travelled

3 What letters come before /ɪd/?

4 🔊 74 Listen and repeat the verbs in the table.

5 🔊 75 Listen and repeat the sentences.
1 I watched a film last night.
2 I played football on Saturday.
3 We visited London last year.
4 We travelled by train.
5 I helped my mum yesterday.

Unit 7
Schwa /ə/

Letters in unstressed syllables
We pronounce some letters in unstressed syllables as /ə/. We call this sound 'schwa'.

1 🔊 76 Listen and repeat the sound /ə/.

2 🔊 77 Listen to the jobs. Where do you hear /ə/?
1 singer
2 lawyer
3 doctor
4 accountant
5 receptionist
6 photographer

3 Listen again and repeat the words.

4 🔊 78 Listen to the sentences. How many times do you hear /ə/ in each sentence?
1 She's a lawyer.
2 He's a good doctor.
3 My brother's an actor.
4 I'd like to be a teacher.

Unit 8
will

Contracted form
We usually use *will* in the contracted form *'ll*.

1 🔊 79 Listen and repeat the contractions.

> I'll   you'll   he'll   she'll   we'll   they'll

2 🔊 80 Listen to the contractions in complete sentences and repeat.
1 I'll see you at 8 o'clock.
2 She'll be here in 10 minutes.

3 🔊 81 Listen. Do you hear a or b?
1 a I go by bus.   b I'll go by bus.
2 a We watch TV.   b We'll watch TV.
3 a They do sports.   b They'll do sports.
4 a You live in the city.   b You'll live in the city.
5 a I speak English.   b I'll speak English.

4 Listen to the answers again and repeat.

5 Work in pairs. Say a sentence in exercise 3. Can your partner tell which you are saying (a or b)?

117

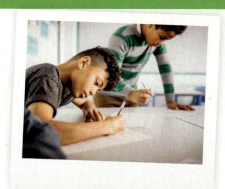

Project planner

Unit 1 Graphic organiser

How to present ideas
- Speak **slowly** and **clearly**.
- **Don't read!**
- Look at **your classmates** when you speak.
- **Pause** after each sentence. Give your classmates time to understand.
- Point to your **visual material** to help your classmates understand.

Unit 2 Graphic organiser

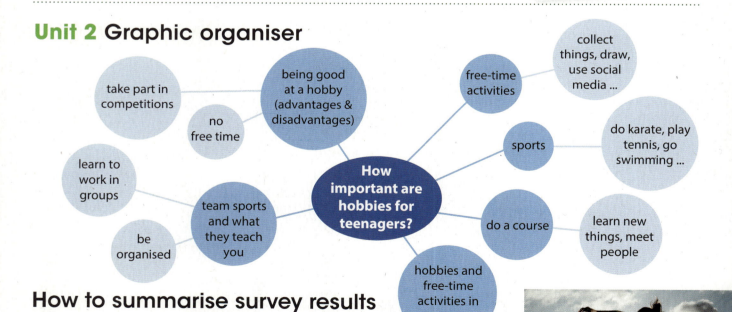

How to summarise survey results
- Give your summary a **clear title**.
- Organise your summary in **clear paragraphs**.
- Use **appropriate language** (*Most people … People always/usually/sometimes …*)
- **Be specific** about numbers (*Six people … Only four people …*)
- Give **examples** (*The most popular … is …*)

Project planner

Unit 3 Graphic organiser

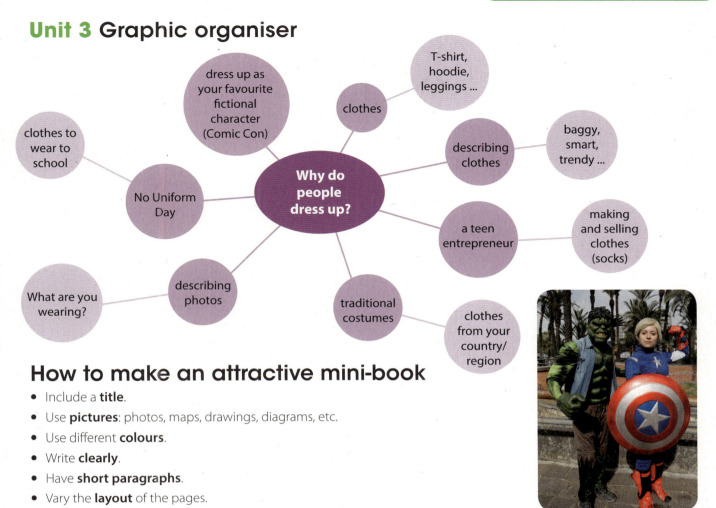

How to make an attractive mini-book
- Include a **title**.
- Use **pictures**: photos, maps, drawings, diagrams, etc.
- Use different **colours**.
- Write **clearly**.
- Have **short paragraphs**.
- Vary the **layout** of the pages.

Unit 4 Graphic organiser

How to make a video
- Record your video in a **light place**.
- Make sure that there isn't a lot of extra **noise**.
- **Stand still** when you speak.
- Look at the camera – and **smile**!
- Speak **loudly** and **clearly**.
- **Pause** between different sections.

119

Project planner

Unit 5 Graphic organiser

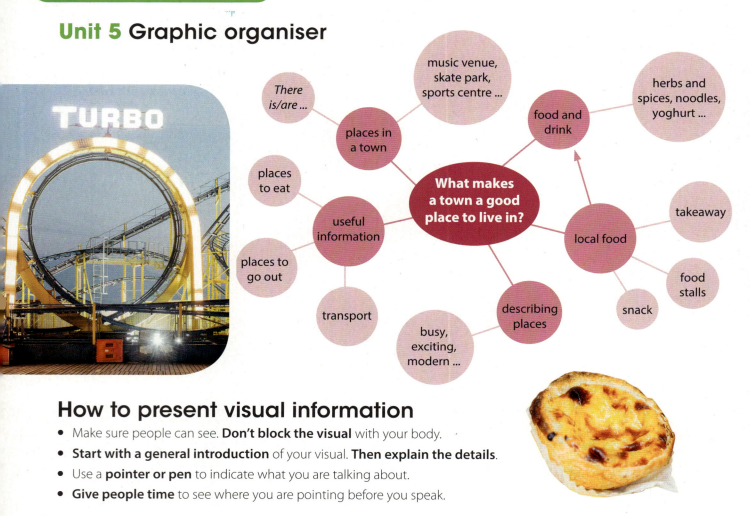

How to present visual information

- Make sure people can see. **Don't block the visual** with your body.
- **Start with a general introduction** of your visual. **Then explain the details**.
- Use a **pointer or pen** to indicate what you are talking about.
- **Give people time** to see where you are pointing before you speak.

Unit 6 Graphic organiser

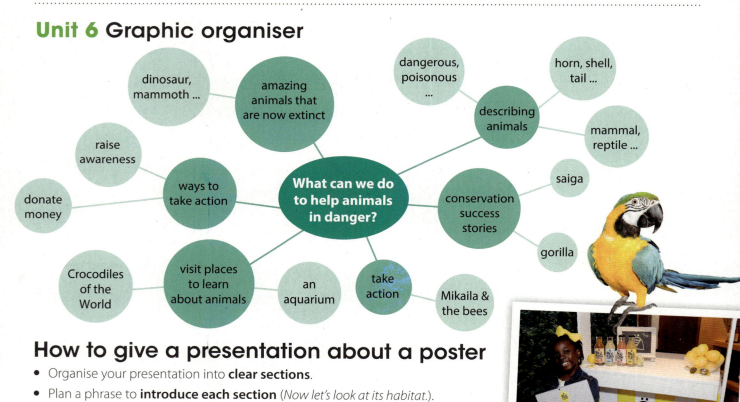

How to give a presentation about a poster

- Organise your presentation into **clear sections**.
- Plan a phrase to **introduce each section** (Now let's look at its habitat.).
- **Decide** who's saying each part.
- **Take your time**: it isn't a problem to pause. People need time to listen and understand.

Project planner

Unit 7 Graphic organiser

- teens rescuing neighbours during Storm Harvey
- local heroes
- superheroes and their day jobs
- Superman – a journalist
- celebrity heroes
- Emma Watson
- generous, kind, polite ...
- adjectives to describe people
- **What makes a hero?**
- making a robot hand
- teen heroes
- writing poetry
- giving opinions (about sports stars)
- sportspeople, heroes from the past
- sending glasses to people who need them

How to make a digital presentation

- Start with a **picture** and/or **questions** to get people interested.
- Use **titles** on each page.
- Have a **picture** on each slide.
- Don't write all the information that you want to say. Have **simple facts**.
- Prepare what you want to say with each slide. Write **notes** that can help you to remember.
- **Practise** what you want to say.

Unit 8 Graphic organiser

- B & B, campsite, youth hostel ...
- go on a city break
- go to the beach
- go to a theme park resort
- types of holiday
- places to stay
- bike hire, games room, swimming pool ...
- Virtual Reality travelling
- in the future
- **What's your idea of a good holiday?**
- facilities
- hang out with friends
- holidays in space
- have a barbecue
- activities to do in the holidays
- go sightseeing

How to indicate the steps of your presentation

- Start with a **clear introduction** to explain what your presentation is about (*I'm going to talk about ...*)
- Use words like *first*, *after that* and *finally* so listeners know you're moving to a new point.
- Give an opportunity for **listeners to ask questions**.
- At the end, **thank people for listening**.

121

Phrasebook

Unit 1 Working together to check answers

Asking about a question
- What about number … ?
- What have you got for number … ?
- Do you think it's … ?

Giving your answer
- I've got …
- I think it's …

Agreeing on the same answer
- Yes, me too.
- You're right.

Disagreeing (you have a different answer)
- Really? I've got …
- Are you sure?

Saying you don't know the answer
- I don't know.

 US → UK Words from the unit

math → maths	I've got math (US) / maths (UK) homework to do.
class → lesson	Do you have a French class (US) / lesson (UK) now?
movie → film	We are watching a good movie (US) / film (UK) at school.

Unit 2 Asking for information
- I'd like to find out about your courses, please.
- Can you tell me about your photography course?
- What time does it start?
- How much is it?
- Do you have a … course?
- Can I sign up for it?
- What day is it on?

 US → UK Words from the unit

soccer → football	I play soccer (US) / football (UK).
practice (verb) → practise	My sister practices (US) / practises (UK) the piano with a teacher.
Do you have … ? → Have you got … ?	Do you have (US) / Have you got (UK) a photography course?

122

Phrasebook

Unit 3 Shopping for clothes

- Do you need any help?
- I'm/We're just looking, thanks.
- I'm looking for (a sweater/some jeans).
- How much is it/are they?
- Can I try it/them on, please?
- The changing rooms are over there.
- It's/They're a bit (small/big/tight/baggy).
- What size is it/are they?
- Have you got this/these in a (small/medium/large)?
- I'll take it/them.

 US → UK Words from the unit

pants → trousers	These pants (US) / trousers (UK) are too tight for you.
sneakers → trainers	I love my new sneakers (US) / trainers (UK)! They're great for running.
purse → handbag	I'm looking for a purse (US) / handbag (UK).

Unit 4 Making and responding to suggestions

Making suggestions

- We should (go by train).
- Let's (get the bus).
- Why don't we (take a picnic)?
- How about (getting the 9:00 bus)?

Agreeing with suggestions

- OK, fine.
- Good idea.

Disagreeing with suggestions

- Really? That's too early.
- I'm not sure. I don't like (picnics).

 US → UK Words from the unit

fall → autumn	Fall (US) / Autumn (UK) is always a rainy and windy season in my country.
awesome → brilliant	This looks awesome (US) / brilliant (UK)!
sunscreen → sun cream	Don't forget to use a hat and sunscreen (US) / sun cream (UK) today – it's very hot.

Phrasebook

Unit 5 Asking for directions

Asking for directions

- Excuse me. Can you tell me how to get to the (library)?
- Is there a (library) near here?

Giving directions

- Go straight ahead.
- Turn left/right.
- Go past the (skate park).
- It's on your left/right.

 US → UK Words from the unit

fries → chips	On Friday night, I sometimes have a burger and some fries (US) / chips (UK) with my friends.
candy → sweets	Eating candy (US) / sweets (UK) isn't good for your teeth.
jelly → jam	My typical breakfast is jelly (US) / jam (UK) on toast.
(movie) theater → cinema	Why don't we go to see a movie at the theater (US) / cinema (UK) this weekend?
subway → underground	Is there a subway (US) / an underground (UK) station near here?

Unit 6 Showing interest

Asking questions

- What was it like?
- Was it fun?

Responding

- You're (kidding/joking)!
- Really? No way!
- That's so funny!
- That's (amazing/cute/great)!
- Sounds (boring/interesting/incredible)!

 US → UK Words from the unit

colorful → colourful	The peacock's feathers are very colorful (US) / colourful (UK).
organization → organisation	She is a volunteer for a wildlife organization (US) / organisation (UK).
meter → metre	Steller's sea cows were up to 9 meters (US) / metres (UK) long.
traveled → travelled	I traveled (US) / travelled (UK) by plane to Spain last year.

Phrasebook

Unit 7 Giving opinions

Asking for opinions
- What do you think of … ?
- What about … ?

Giving opinions
- I (don't) think …
- If you ask me, …

Agreeing
- Yes, I think you're right about that.
- You've got a point.

Disagreeing
- No way!
- That's ridiculous.

 US ➔ UK Words from the unit

neighbor ➔ neighbour   The teen heroes helped rescue their neighbors (US) / neighbours (UK).

Unit 8 Making arrangements

- What are you doing Saturday?
- What are you up to Saturday?
- Nothing special. Why?
- I can't Saturday morning. I'm …
- Are you free in the afternoon?
- How about Saturday morning?
- Yes, I think so. / No, sorry, I'm …
- Are you doing anything Sunday?
- I'm busy Sunday morning.
- I'm free in the afternoon.

 **US ➔ UK** Words from the unit

parking lot ➔ car park   There's a parking lot (US) / car park (UK) near the supermarket – we can leave the car there.
vacation ➔ holiday   My family and I went on vacation (US) / holiday (UK) to Brazil last summer.
two thirty ➔ half past two   Let's meet at two thirty (US) / half past two (UK).

125

Irregular verbs

Infinitive	Past simple	Past participle
be /biː/	was/were /wɒz/ /wɜː(r)/	been /biːn/
become /bɪˈkʌm/	became /bɪˈkeɪm/	become /bɪˈkʌm/
begin /bɪˈɡɪn/	began /bɪˈɡæn/	begun /bɪˈɡʌn/
break /breɪk/	broke /brəʊk/	broken /ˈbrəʊkən/
bring /brɪŋ/	brought /brɔːt/	brought /brɔːt/
build /bɪld/	built /bɪlt/	built /bɪlt/
buy /baɪ/	bought /bɔːt/	bought /bɔːt/
catch /kætʃ/	caught /kɔːt/	caught /kɔːt/
choose /tʃuːz/	chose /tʃəʊz/	chosen /ˈtʃəʊz(ə)n/
come /kʌm/	came /keɪm/	come /kʌm/
cut /kʌt/	cut /kʌt/	cut /kʌt/
do /duː/	did /dɪd/	done /dʌn/
drink /drɪŋk/	drank /dræŋk/	drunk /drʌŋk/
drive /draɪv/	drove /drəʊv/	driven /ˈdrɪv(ə)n/
eat /iːt/	ate /eɪt/	eaten /ˈiːt(ə)n/
fall /fɔːl/	fell /fel/	fallen /ˈfɔːlən/
feed /fiːd/	fed /fed/	fed /fed/
feel /fiːl/	felt /felt/	felt /felt/
find /faɪnd/	found /faʊnd/	found /faʊnd/
fly /flaɪ/	flew /fluː/	flown /fləʊn/
forget /fə(r)ˈɡet/	forgot /fə(r)ˈɡɒt/	forgotten /fə(r)ˈɡɒt(ə)n/
get /ɡet/	got /ɡɒt/	got /ɡɒt/
give /ɡɪv/	gave /ɡeɪv/	given /ˈɡɪv(ə)n/
go /ɡəʊ/	went /went/	gone /ɡɒn/
grow /ɡrəʊ/	grew /ɡruː/	grown /ɡrəʊn/
hang /hæŋ/	hung /hʌŋ/	hung /hʌŋ/
have /hæv/	had /hæd/	had /hæd/
hear /hɪə(r)/	heard /hɜː(r)d/	heard /hɜː(r)d/
hit /hɪt/	hit /hɪt/	hit /hɪt/
keep /kiːp/	kept /kept/	kept /kept/
know /nəʊ/	knew /njuː/	known /nəʊn/

Irregular verbs

Infinitive	Past simple	Past participle
lay /leɪ/	laid /leɪd/	laid /leɪd/
learn /lɜː(r)n/	learnt/learned /lɜː(r)nt/ /lɜː(r)nd/	learnt/learned /lɜː(r)nt/ /lɜː(r)nd/
leave /liːv/	left /left/	left /left/
let /let/	let /let/	let /let/
lose /luːz/	lost /lɒst/	lost /lɒst/
make /meɪk/	made /meɪd/	made /meɪd/
meet /miːt/	met /met/	met /met/
pay /peɪ/	paid /peɪd/	paid /peɪd/
put /pʊt/	put /pʊt/	put /pʊt/
read /riːd/	read /red/	read /red/
ride /raɪd/	rode /rəʊd/	ridden /ˈrɪd(ə)n/
ring /rɪŋ/	rang /ræŋ/	rung /rʌŋ/
run /rʌn/	ran /ræn/	run /rʌn/
say /seɪ/	said /sed/	said /sed/
see /siː/	saw /sɔː/	seen /siːn/
sell /sel/	sold /səʊld/	sold /səʊld/
send /send/	sent /sent/	sent /sent/
shine /ʃaɪn/	shone /ʃɒn/	shone /ʃɒn/
sing /sɪŋ/	sang /sæŋ/	sung /sʌŋ/
sit /sɪt/	sat /sæt/	sat /sæt/
sleep /sliːp/	slept /slept/	slept /slept/
speak /spiːk/	spoke /spəʊk/	spoken /ˈspəʊkən/
spend /spend/	spent /spent/	spent /spent/
sweep /swiːp/	swept /swept/	swept /swept/
swim /swɪm/	swam /swæm/	swum /swʌm/
take /teɪk/	took /tʊk/	taken /ˈteɪkən/
teach /tiːtʃ/	taught /tɔːt/	taught /tɔːt/
tell /tel/	told /təʊld/	told /təʊld/
think /θɪŋk/	thought /θɔːt/	thought /θɔːt/
throw /θrəʊ/	threw /θruː/	thrown /θrəʊn/
understand /ˌʌndə(r)ˈstænd/	understood /ˌʌndə(r)ˈstʊd/	understood /ˌʌndə(r)ˈstʊd/
wake /weɪk/	woke /wəʊk/	woken /ˈwəʊkən/
win /wɪn/	won /wʌn/	won /wʌn/
write /raɪt/	wrote /rəʊt/	written /ˈrɪt(ə)n/

Macmillan Education Limited
4 Crinan Street
London N1 9XW

Companies and representatives throughout the world

Get Involved! Student's Book A2 ISBN 978-1-380-06491-2
Get Involved! Student's Book A2 with Student's App and Digital Student's Book ISBN 978-1-380-06879-8

Text © Gill Holley, Catherine McBeth, Kate Pickering, Patricia Reilly 2021
Design and illustration © Macmillan Education Limited 2021

The authors have asserted their right to be identified as the authors of this work in accordance with the Copyright, Designs and Patents Act 1988.

First published 2021

All rights reserved. No part of this publication may be reproduced, stored in a retrieval system, or transmitted in any form or by any means, electronic, mechanical, photocopying, recording, or otherwise, without the prior written permission of the publishers.

Original design by Designers Educational Ltd and emc design ltd
Page make-up by Wild Apple Design Ltd
Illustrated by Alexandra Barboza (Lemonade Illustration Agency) p89; Esther Cuadrado (Beehive Illustration) p40; Daniela Geremia (Beehive Illustration) pp13, 64, 114; David Hurtado (Beehive Illustration) pp48, 49, 65, 71; Tamara Joubert (Beehive Illustration) p56; Peter Lubach (Beehive Illustration) p7; Camille Medina (Beehive Illustration) p17; Jim Peacock (Beehive Illustration) p9; Martin Sanders (Beehive Illustration) p67; Kate Sheppard (Beehive Illustration) pp19, 52
Cover design by Designers Educational Ltd
Cover photograph by Getty Images/Tony Anderson, Getty Images/martinedoucet, Getty Images/Maskot, Getty Images/Pollyana Ventura
Picture research by Catherine Dunn
Cover image research by Penelope Bowden, Proudfoot Pictures

Authors' acknowledgements
Gill would like to thank her friends from International House, Barcelona.
Kate would like to thank all her colleagues and friends at International House, Madrid.

The authors and publishers would like to thank the following for permission to reproduce their photographs:
Airbus p100; **Alamy** pp43(jacket), 108(C), Alamy/CBP Photo p87(t), Alamy/leonello calvetti p74, Alamy/Mike Cavaroc p88(bl), Alamy/Ian Dagnall p68(tl), Alamy/Danita Delimont p12(br), Alamy/Richard Green p39(E), Alamy/Graham Jepson p24(tr), Alamy/Natalia Klenova p37(E), Alamy/Ruslan Kudrin p41(D), Alamy/Marisa Lia p41(B), Alamy/Fco Javier Rivas Martín p39(F), Alamy/Moodboard p25(cl), Alamy/Malcolm Park p39(G), Alamy/Helene Rogers p36(B), Alamy/Mark Shahaf p66, Alamy/Wdnet Studio pp15(tl), 118(cr), Alamy/titoOnz p48(background), Alamy/Xinhua p87(bl); **Anthony Byrne** pp11, 38, 39(D); **Bananastock** pp53(cl), 103(trb); **Betjamin Poetry Prize** p89(6); **Digital Vision** pp73(6), 78(tr); **g4g.co.uk** p75(cr); **Getty** pp10(3, 6), 14(A, H), 23(A), 54(background), 53(I, J), 61(5), 63(br), 64(cake, cheese, fish, milk, peas), 73(5), 76(br, boy, fossil), 96(4, 7), 108(E), 112(tl), 112(sports live, future world), 120(cake), Getty/G15702993 p60(4), Getty/1001nights p47(cl, cr), Getty/adamkaz p112(tr), Getty/AFP p87(br), Getty/Anadolu Agency pp11(8), 16, Getty/AndreyPopov p32(tl), Getty/Artisteer p89(5), Getty/Thomas Barwick pp24(tr), 118(br) Getty/Believe_In_Me p41(E), Getty/Bet Noire p112(news update), Getty/Bhofack2 pp60(2), 115, Getty/Birdland p25(2), Getty/Boston Globe p80(tl), Getty/Juan Jose Lopez Brotons pp22-23, Getty/Cmcderm 1 p10(4), Getty/d3sign/Moment p3(cr), Getty/David Cabrera p68(c), 120(tr), Getty/Kryissa Campos p72(peacock), Getty/Custom Designer pp53(D), 119(bl), Getty/DGLimages p8(C), Getty/daitoZen p60(1), Getty/Danicek p53(E), Getty/Dado Daniela p114, Getty/Dean Conger pp11(3), 50, 51(bl), 119(cr), Getty/David Wall Photo p46(background), Getty/Donna Day p79(tr), Getty/Elitsia Deykova p99(tl), Getty/Jerry Driendl pp101(1), 121(br), Getty/Duci86 p90, Getty/David De Lossy p29(hockey), Getty/Steve Debenport p35, Getty/Domin_domin p53(E, F), Getty/Donaldson Collection p95(1), Getty/Dorling Kindersley p89(4), Getty/Richard Drury p104(Jake), Getty/Dulezidar p61(7), Getty/Sam Edwards p41(tr), Getty/Envirionmantic p63(bl), Getty Images/EyeEm p68(tr), Getty/Eyewire p31(trl), Getty/Don Farrall p72(bee), Getty/FatCamera p8(B), Getty/Fotografo p54, Getty/Ana Francisconi p37(H), Getty/Fuse p101(5), Getty/Gbh007 p101(3), Getty/Aurelian Gogonea p73(4), Getty/Dinoco Greco p14(B), Getty/Green_Leaf p41(C), Getty/Judith Haeusler p101(4), Getty/Hero Images pp14(I), 18(tr), 104(Ian), 108(F), Getty Images/iStockphoto p112(travel tips, tech news), Getty/Itsabreeze Photography p73(3), Getty/Ivanastar p89(3), Getty/jewhyte p107(b), Getty/jirawatp p94-95(background), Getty/Johnner Images p14(C), Getty/Hugh Johnston p79(tr), Getty/I. Jonsson p41(G), Getty/Beverley Joubert p99(tr), Getty/Sharoncudworth p112(teen talk), Getty/Simala Kama p108(G), Getty/Keeweeboy p10(7), Getty/Kirby p92(tr), Getty/Victor Kitaykin p53(K), Getty/Mitchell Krog p75(tr), Getty/Chalermphon Kumchai p17(tl), Getty/Minoru Kuriyama p96(6), Getty/LauriPatterson p63(tr), Getty/Sandra Leidholdt p72(goat), Getty/Lenta p37(G), Getty/Ljupco p36(C), Getty/Lonely Planet Images p107(tr), Getty/Malerapaso p53(B), Getty/MamiGibbs p6(br), Getty/Manakin p53(C), Getty/MarisaLia p115(pasta), Getty/MediaProduction p41(H), Getty/Miodrag Ignjatovic p23(C), Getty/Montecello pp53(A), 61(bl), Getty/Image by Catherine MacBride p42, Getty/MachineHeadz p13(tl, cl), Getty/Peeranon Mahanil p84(cockpit), Getty/Turgay Malikili p104(4), Getty/Manakin p53(C), Getty/ManikChauhan p63(tl), Getty/martinedoucet p8(A), Getty/Adriana Marteva p61(6), Getty/mawielobob p43(dress), Getty/MediaProduction p41(H), Getty/Miodrag Ignjatovic p23(C), Getty/Donald Miralle pp2(bl), 27(t), Getty/Ar Duche Misfa'l p104(6), Getty/Moment/d3sign p2(bc), Getty/Montecello p53(A), Getty/NASA p95(3), Getty/Newscast p109(bl), Getty/Thorsten Nilson p83(tl), Getty/Thomas Northcut p32(tr), Getty/Olivia Bell Photography p36(A), Getty/Gary Ombler p73(tr), Getty/oneinchpunch p44(B), Getty/Daniel Osterkamp pp72(background), 73(br), Getty/Oxygen p58, Getty/Pacific Press p88(tr), Getty/Parrotstarr pp73(tr), 120; Getty/Simona Pilolla p10(8), Getty/Poeroforever p29(skating), Getty/Witthaya Prasongsin p85(camera), Getty/Sarote Pruksachat p96(3), Getty/purestock p73(2), Getty/David Ramos pp91(tr), 133(tr), Getty/RazvanChisu pp96(2), 121(br), Getty/Lowell Richards p83(tr), Getty/Riou p108(I), Getty/Rohappy pp44(B), 131(cr), Getty/Lauri Rotko p59(cr), Getty/Roundhill p10(1), Getty/Chris Ryan p103(trr), Getty/Pete Saloutos p36(D), Getty/Carsten Schanter p99(Lucy Lake), Getty/Roy JAMES Shakespeare p25(1), Getty/Sidekick p23(B), Getty/Sitikka p59(tl), Getty/Tim Snell p65, Getty/Solstock pp12, 118(tr), Getty/Alexander Spatari p108(B), Getty/Marie Stone p112(natural science), Getty/Paul Sutherland p79(tr), Getty/Stock Colours p55, Getty/SvetaOrlova p29(aerobics), Getty/Stephen Swintek p101(6), Getty/Bob Stevens p14(E), Getty/James Stone p99(Lucien), Getty/Cordier Sylvain p108(A), Getty/szeyuen pp8(D), 108(A), Getty/Monica and Michael Sweet pp2(turtle), 72(turtle), 115(turtle), Getty/Chris Danielle Tabangay p63(tr), Getty/Burcu Atalay Tankut p60(3), Getty/Tetra Images p14(D, J), Getty/theasis p107(cr), Getty Images/Thinkstock pp77(b), 84(Marvel, news), 109(br), 133(tr), Getty/TimeStopper p85(technology), Getty/Tirc83 p102, Getty/Victor Tyakht p75(bl), Getty/ValuaVitaly p37(F), Getty/Daria Vasenina p37(bl), Getty/Klaus Vedfelt p23(D), Getty/Richard Villalon p53(G), Getty/Visionhaus p91(tll), Getty/Westend61 pp15(tr), 30, 59(cl), 96(5), 103(trl), 112(good cooking), Getty/Kim Westerskov p95(background), Getty/Whitewish p64, Getty/Wwing p53(H), Getty/Poh Kim Yeoh p36(B, I), 103(trl) **Image Source** p10(5); **iStockphoto** pp43, 73(1), 108(D), 115(trainers); **Johner Images** p17(tr); **Macmillan Education Limited** p70-71; **NASA** p95(2); **Antonio Zazueta Olmos** p89(2); **PhotoDisc** pp84(briefcase), 85(chemicals), 96(1), 108(H), **Photofixstudios** p85; **Purestock** p99(Holiday Guy); **Radius Images** p99(Ryan); **Shutterstock** p95(4), Shutterstock/Aratehortua p104(1), Shutterstock/Roberta Basile pp39(C), 119Z(tl), Shutterstock/Boris15 p75(br), Shutterstock/borkiss p41(A), Shutterstock/Carboxylase p104(3), Shutterstock/Amos Chapple p51(cr), Shutterstock/ric Charbonneau p39(B), Shutterstock/Cosmic_Design p104(5), Shutterstock/ESB Professional p80(tr, background), Shutterstock/Peter Hermes Furian p92(background), Shutterstock/gresei pp43, 115(jeans), Shutterstock/Andrea Izzotti p72(dolphin), Shutterstock/Julia Kaysa p10(2), Shutterstock/Kobal pp2(Shuri), 84(Superman, Shuri), 85(Spider-Man), Shutterstock/Mario Laporta p39(A), Shutterstock/Monkey Business Images p14(F, G), Shutterstock/Moviestore pp84(Batman, Marvel), 121(tr), Shutterstock/Evgeniya Porechenskaya pp43, 115(hoodie), Shutterstock/RastoS p52(cr), Shutterstock/Alexander Raths p106(background), Shutterstock/Roger-Viollet p92(cr), Shutterstock/Susan Schmitz p72(snake), Shutterstock/Vasyl Shulga p115(14), Shutterstock/Charles Sykes pp11, 77(br), 120(br), Shutterstock/VectorsMarket p104(2), Shutterstock/wavebreakmedia p31(trr), Shutterstock/TheWonderWays p82(background), Shutterstock/xpixel pp30, 31(tr); **Superstock** pp6(1, 2, 3, 4, 5, 6), 52(bl), 62(Portuguese, Jamaican, Philippines, Thai); **Unlimited Tomorrow** p89(1)

Video footage and stills supplied by:
BBC Studios Ltd pp3, 37, 85; Digeo Productions pp24, 46, 49, 73, 97; DLA pp13, 61; MTJ pp3, 19, 31, 43, 55, 67, 79, 91, 103, 122, 123, 124; Maia Films pp3, 22, 34, 58, 70, 82, 94, 106

Additional sources:
Baldwin, S. (10th April 2014) 'The future of travel: Gareth Williams, Skyscanner CEO predicts', Skyscanner.net

These materials may contain links for third party websites. We have no control over, and are not responsible for, the contents of such third party websites. Please use care when accessing them.

The inclusion of any specific companies, commercial products, trade names or otherwise does not constitute or imply its endorsement or recommendation by Macmillan Education Limited.

Printed and bound in Poland by CGS

2026 2025 2024 2023 2022
30 29 28 27 26 25 24 23 22 21